Chaos & Cosmos

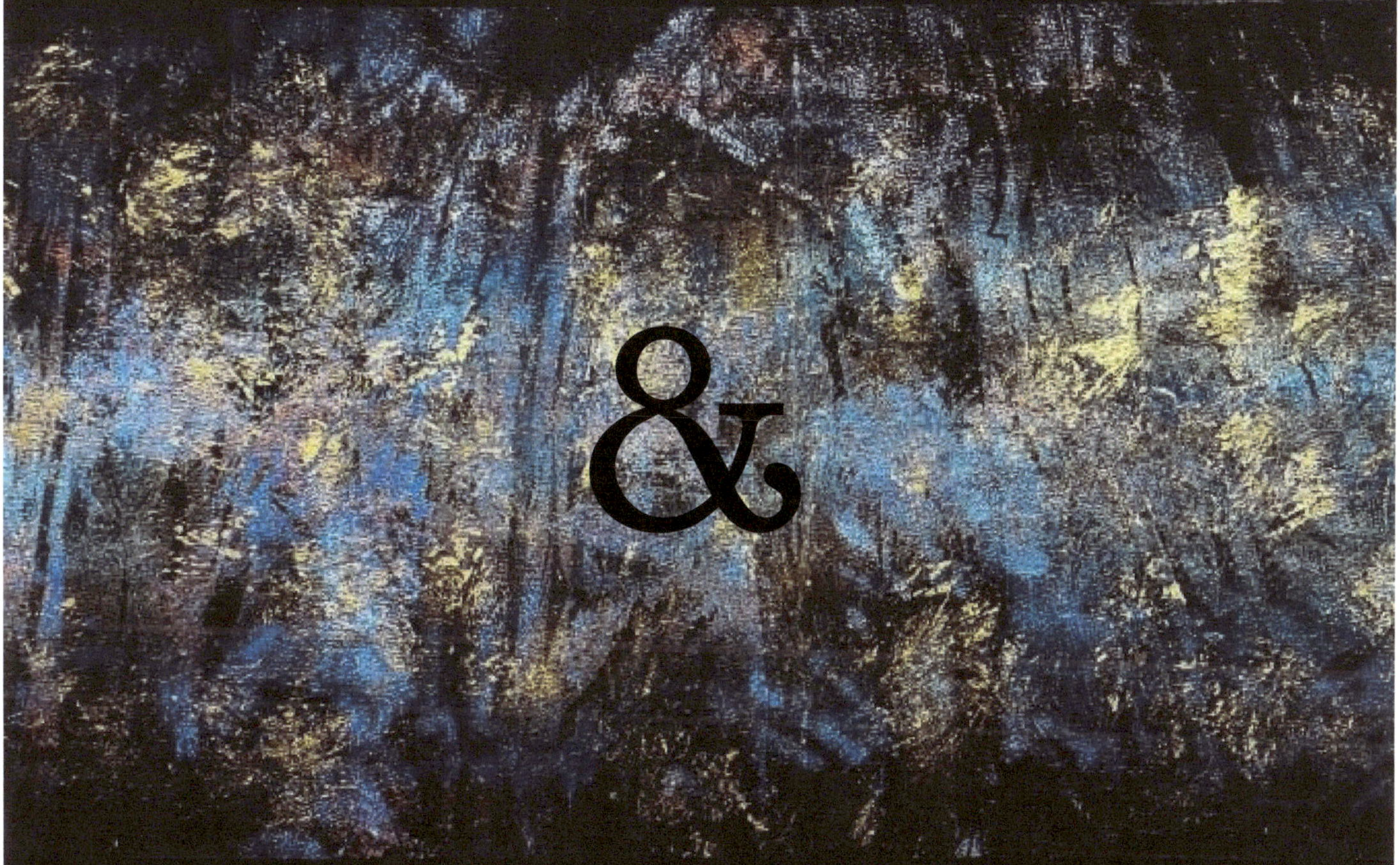

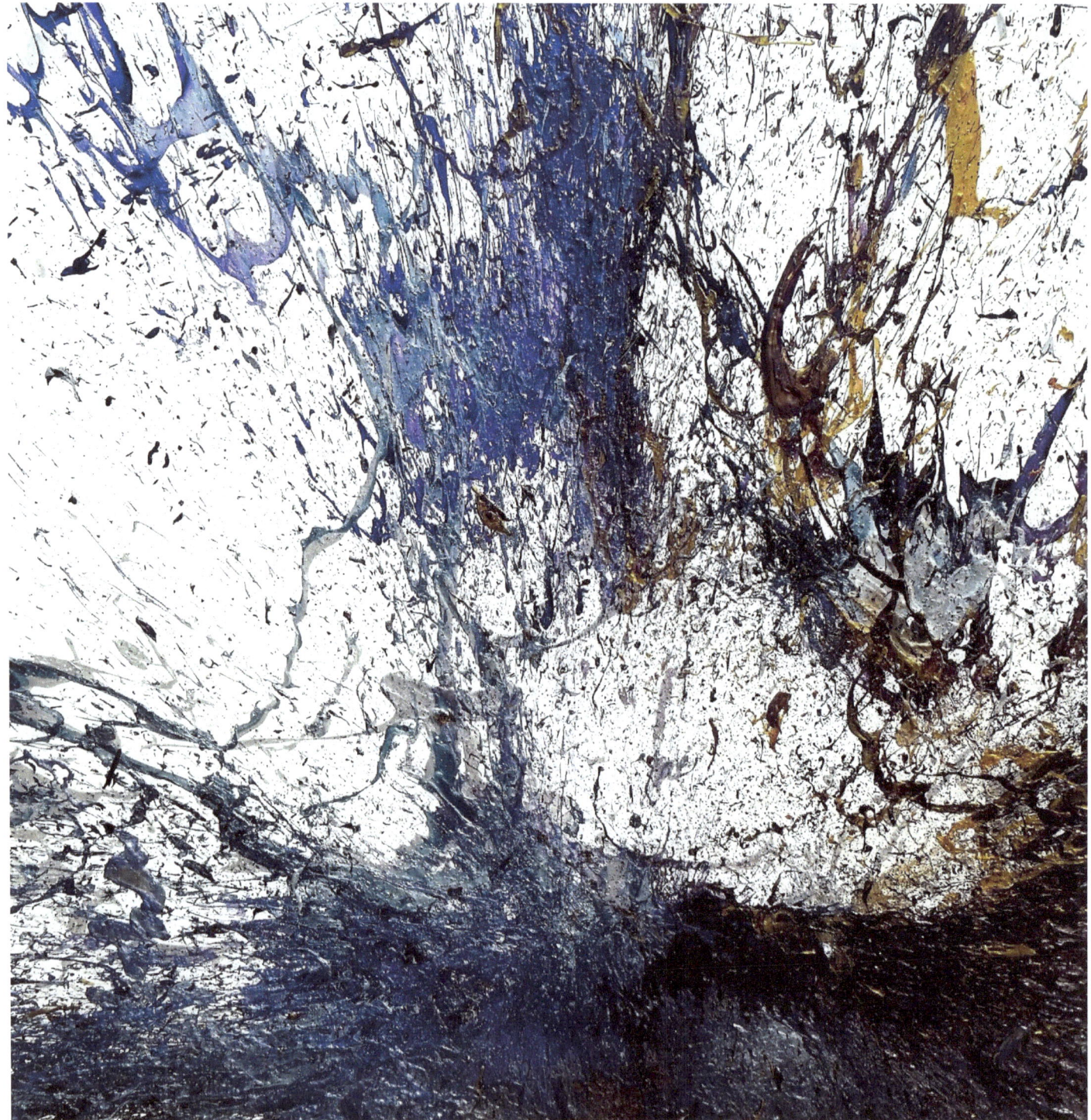

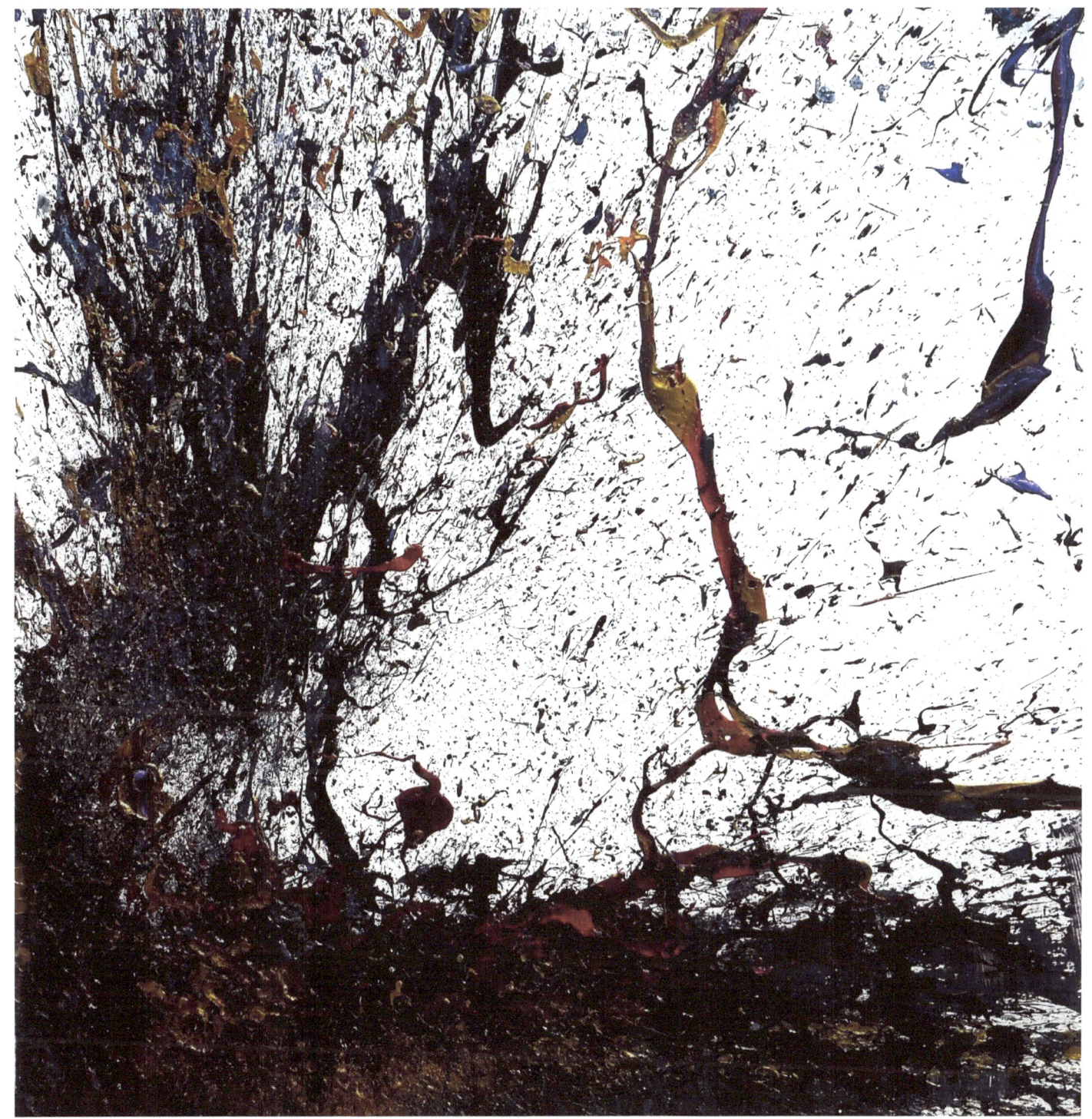

Previous pages: *Matter* (L) and *Anti-matter*

These pieces were created at the same time by placing a coffee filter filled with paint placed where the two boards touched. Each board was angled up slightly to 'cup' the paint squib. A firecracker was used for application.

Opposite page: *Mending Fences*

This was the first piece I ever sold to a stranger. It was created rather on accident, when an explosion didn't go as planned. Instead of trashing the entire piece, I used a credit card like a scraper to spread the paint to the edges. The image always made me think of memories so long past they seem filtered and obscured through the lens of time.

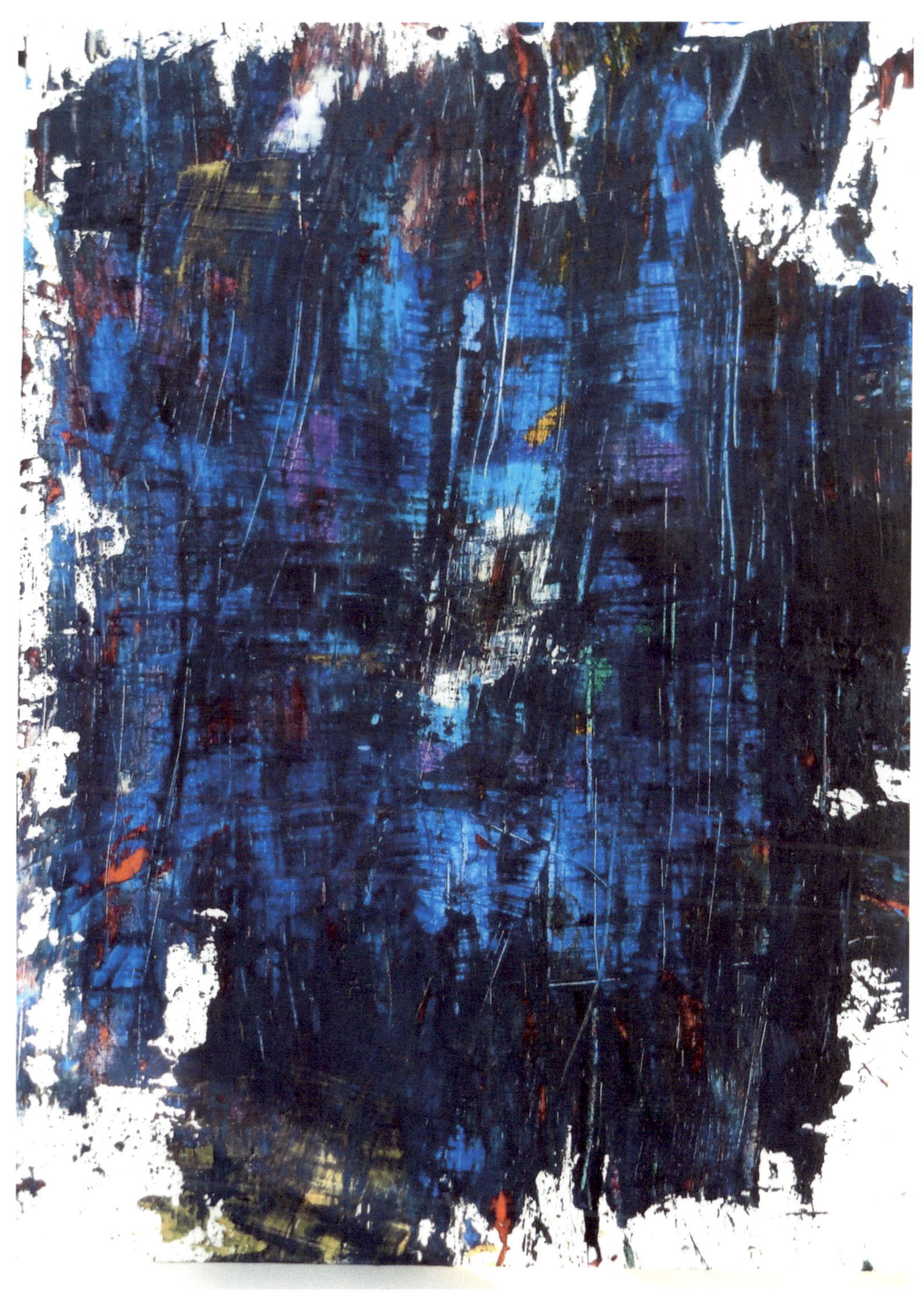

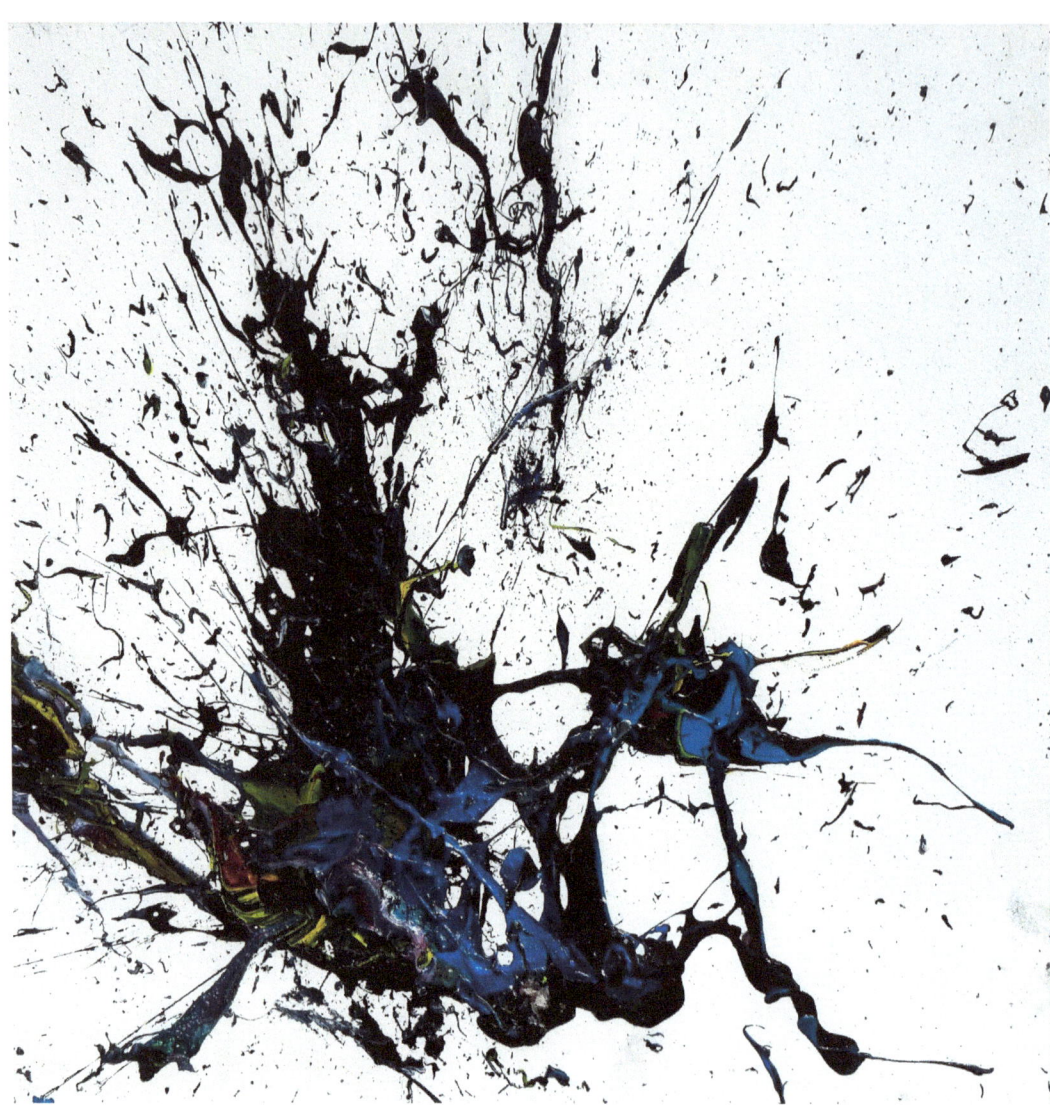

Right: *Mating Dragons,* was created about the same time as *Ampersand Logogram*, although it's placement relative to the coffee filter squib differed dramatically.

Title inspired by the mating practices hypothesized in Discovery Channel's "The Last Dragon."

Above: *Ampersand logogram,* is one of my first paintings. It is cradled gessoboard with a coffee filter squib filled with acrylic paint, applied with a firecracker.

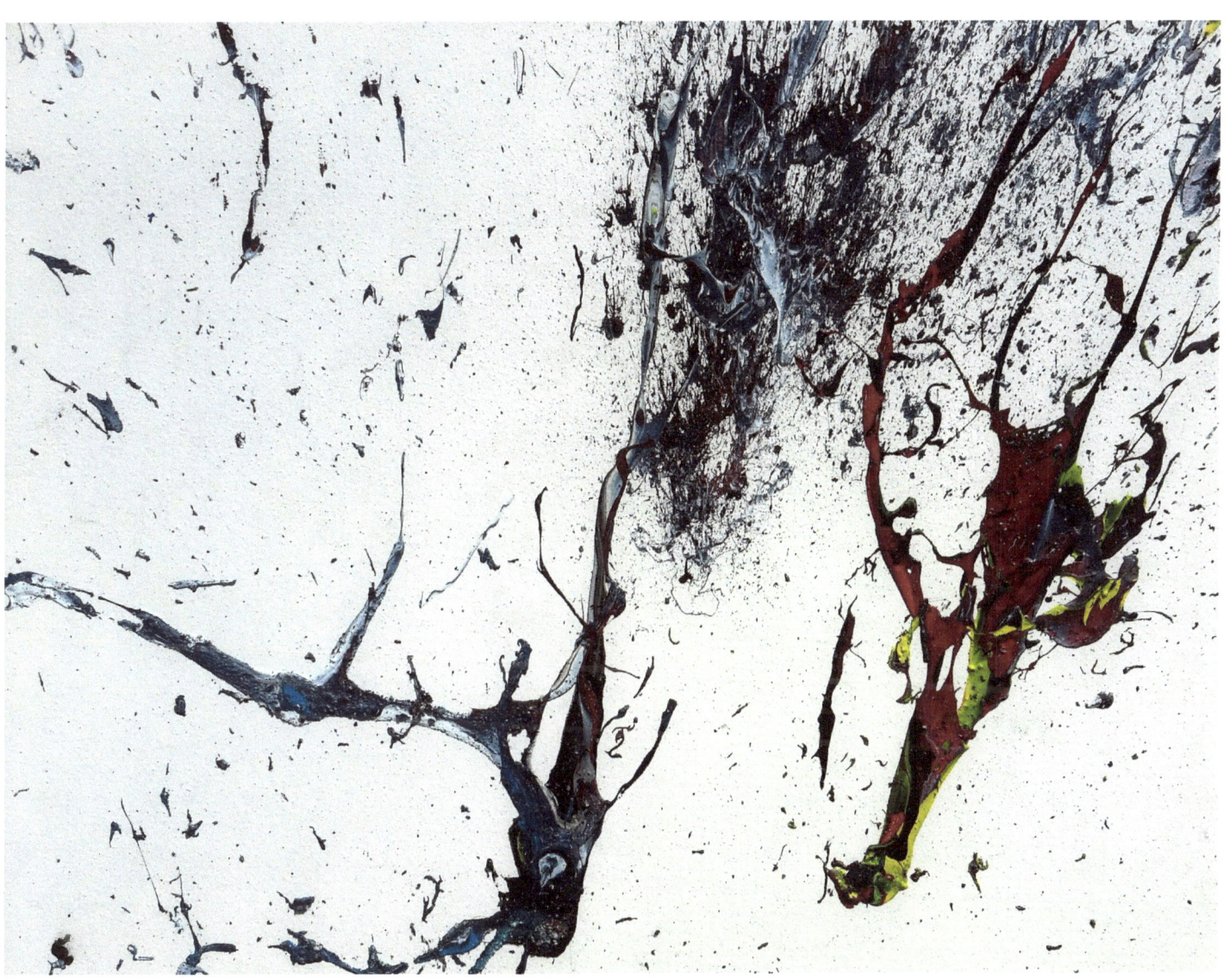

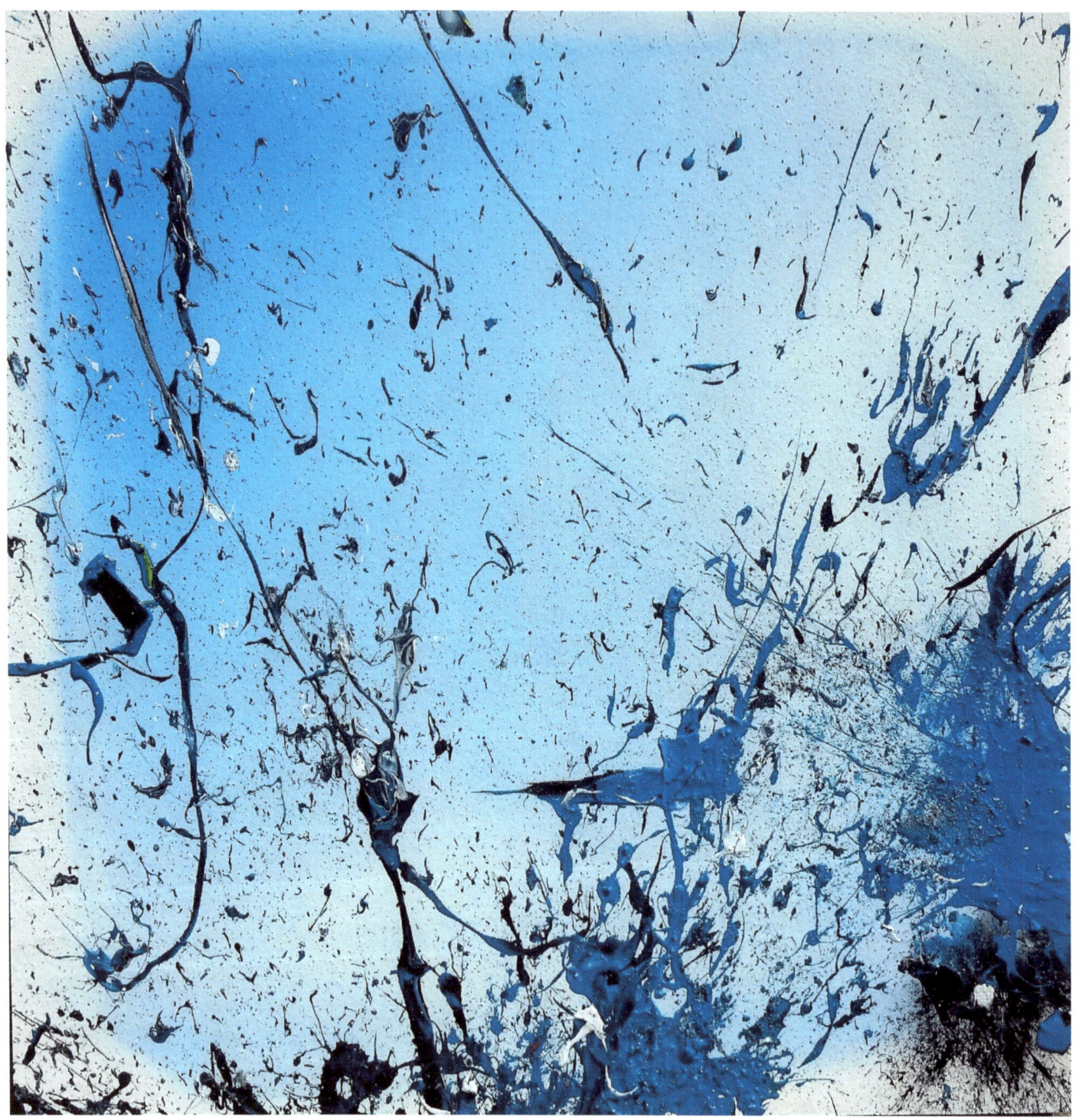

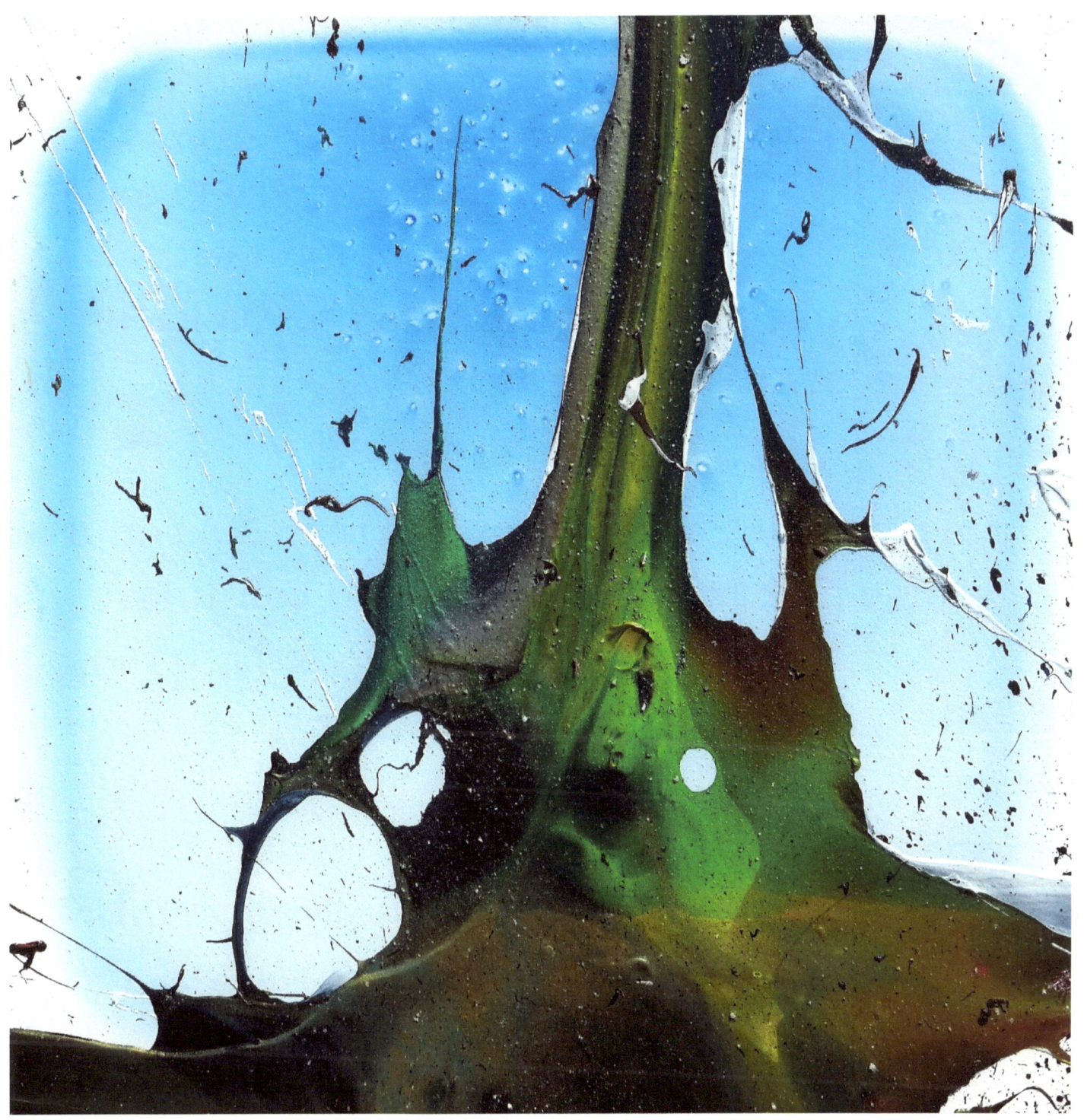

Previous pages: *Blue Tube* (L) and *Coronal Mass Ejection* (R) are both gessoboard with acrylic paint applied with a firecracker. These two also show some earlier experimentation with smoke bombs for tinting boards pre-explosion. Early on, my results tended to vary wildly

Opposite page: *Blast plate* was created around the same time as the previous two paintings. This is one is the first to incorporate both smoke bomb tinting and multiple explosive applications.

Bonus! *Coronal Mass Ejection* and *Blast plate* were two of the first paintings I ever showed publically, in the inaugural Boro Art Crawl!

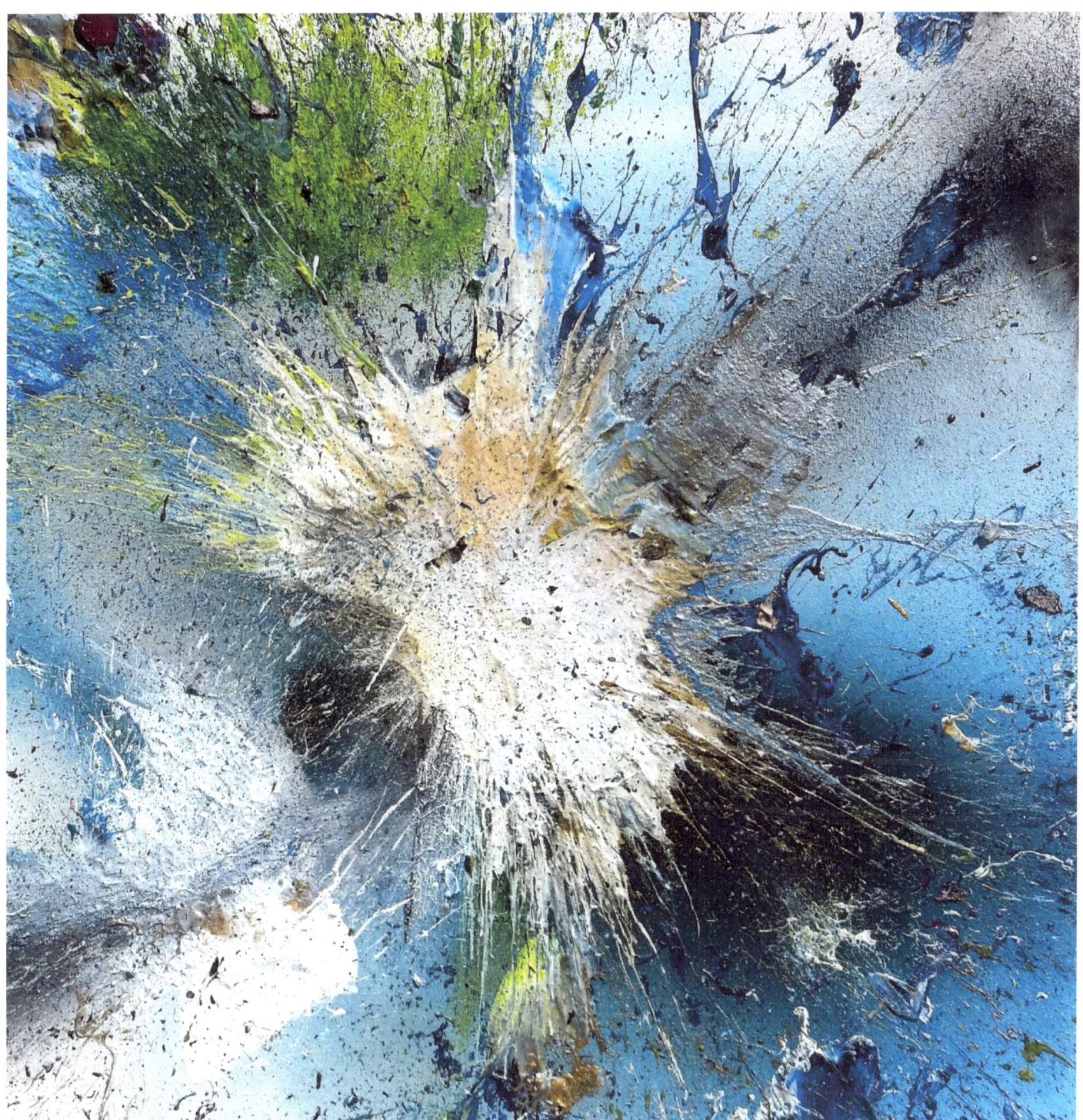

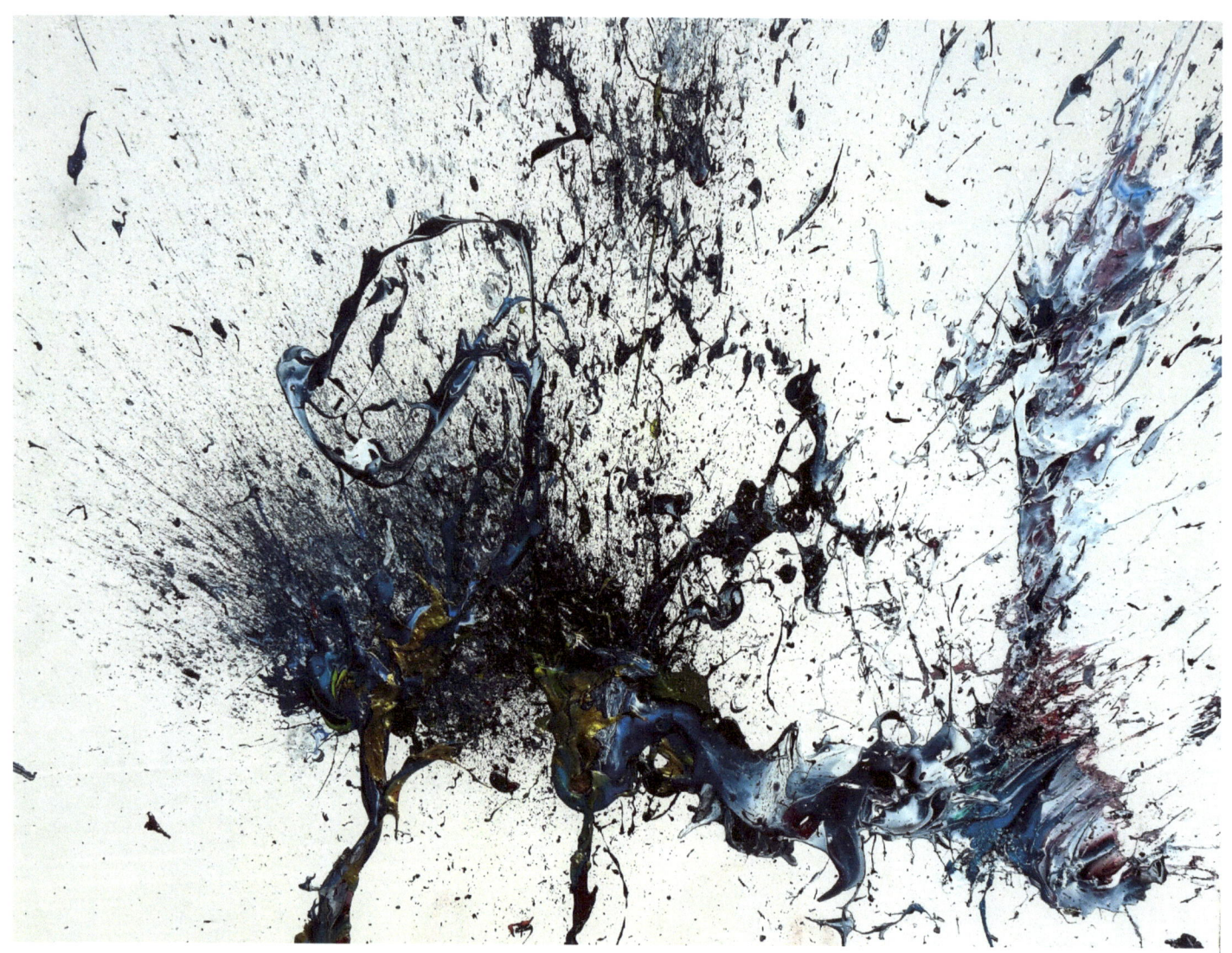

Above: *Entering the burning bush* is another painting created along side *Mating Dragons* and *Ampersand Logogram* (using similar methods). The title is inspired by the idea of the vertical shape to the right being an angel, entering the burning bush, in the center. What? It's **abstract art**, maaaaan.

Right: *Fantasma* was created early on and represents multiple explosive applications of acrylic paint on gessoboard.

The title is a word created/used by myself and my former coworker and good friend, Sam (which is short for **Samicles**).

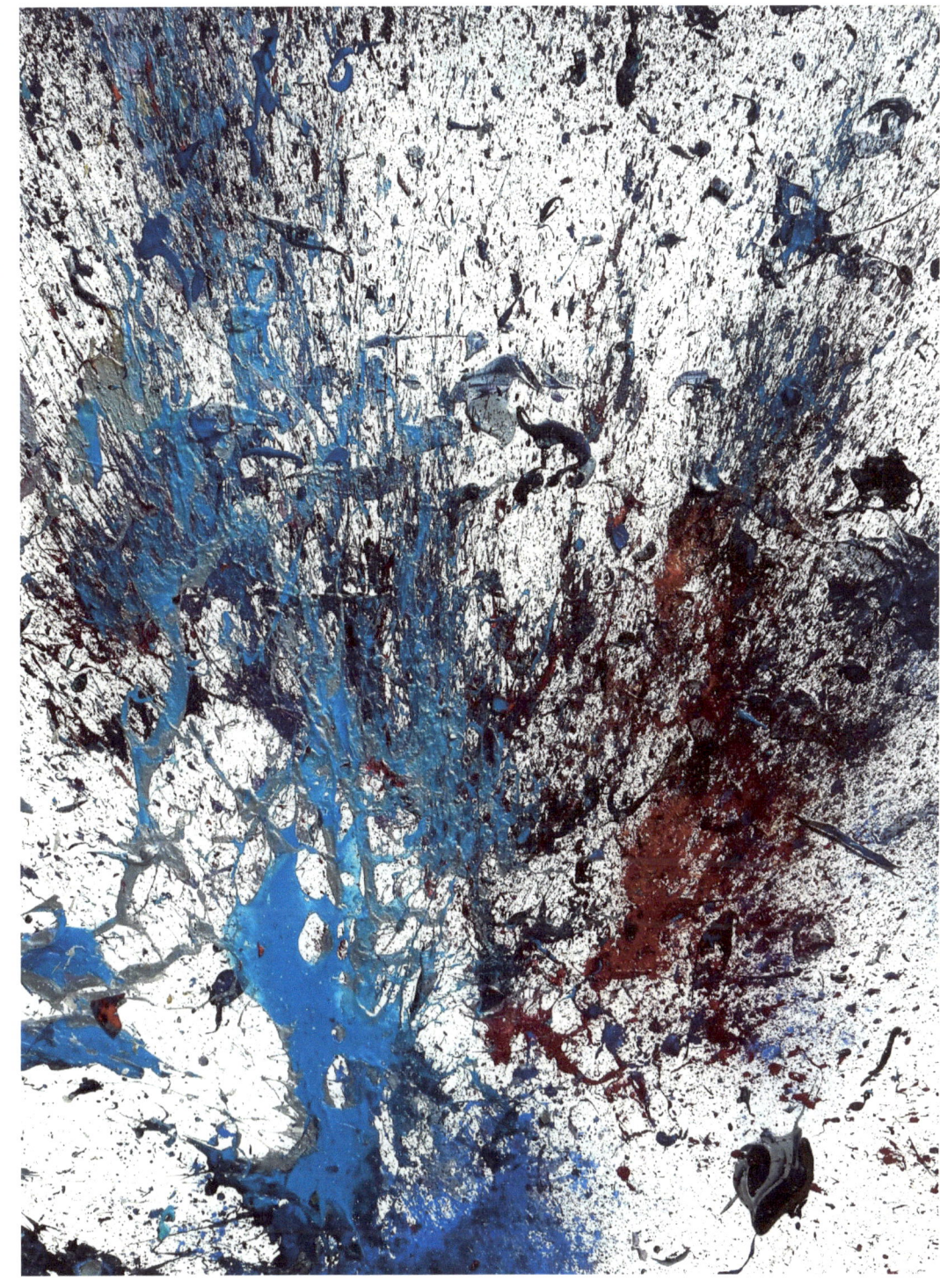

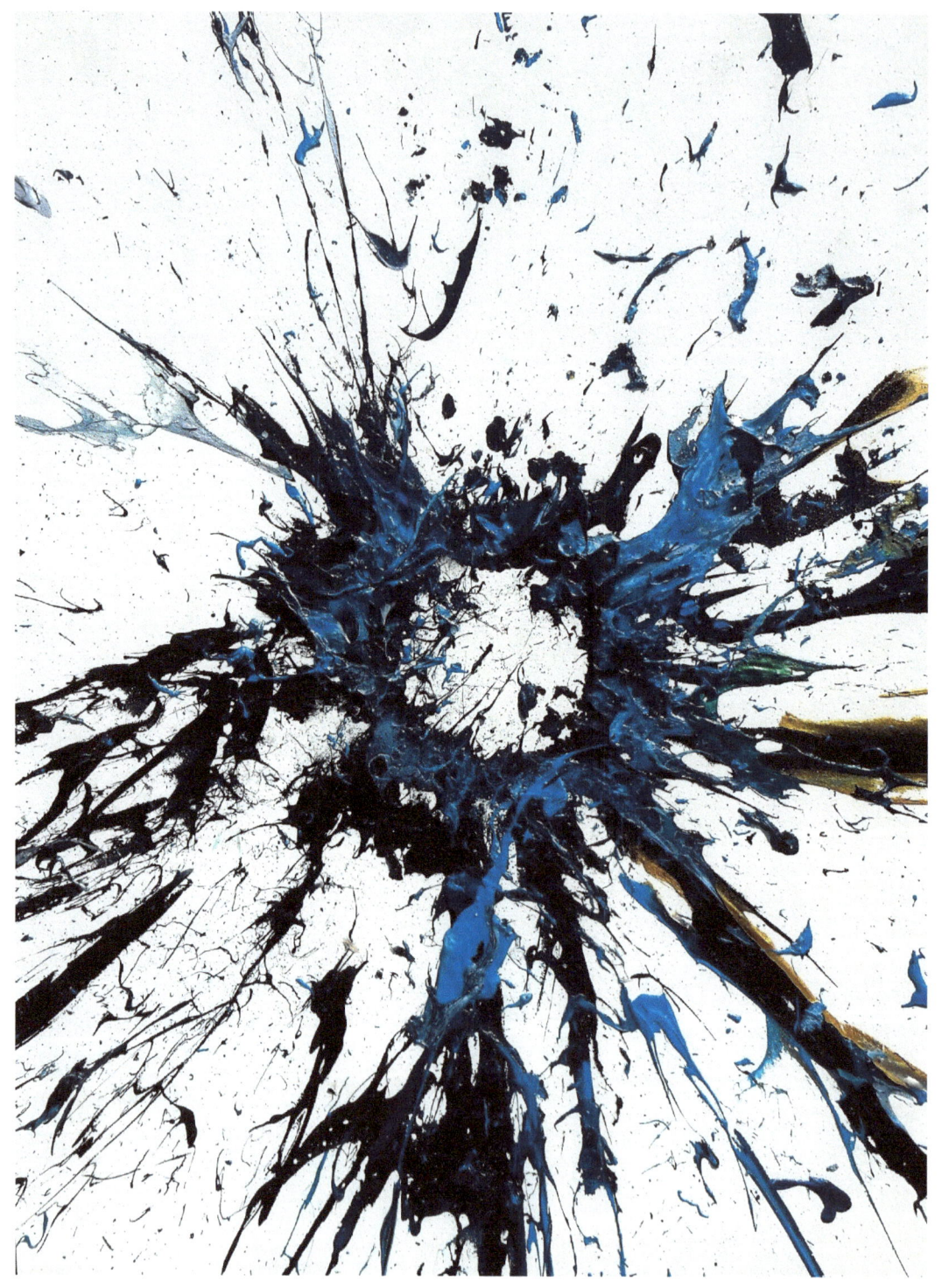

Left: *Cornell's Sun* found me creating the first in series of other *Cornell* titled pieces. The general pattern is highly reproducible. This obtuse reference to 90s rock stings a bit more, since Chris Cornell's suicide.

Below: *Above the deep* gets its title from my listening to too many audiobooks and open courses on the Old Testament leading up to my decision to blow things up and see how it looks.

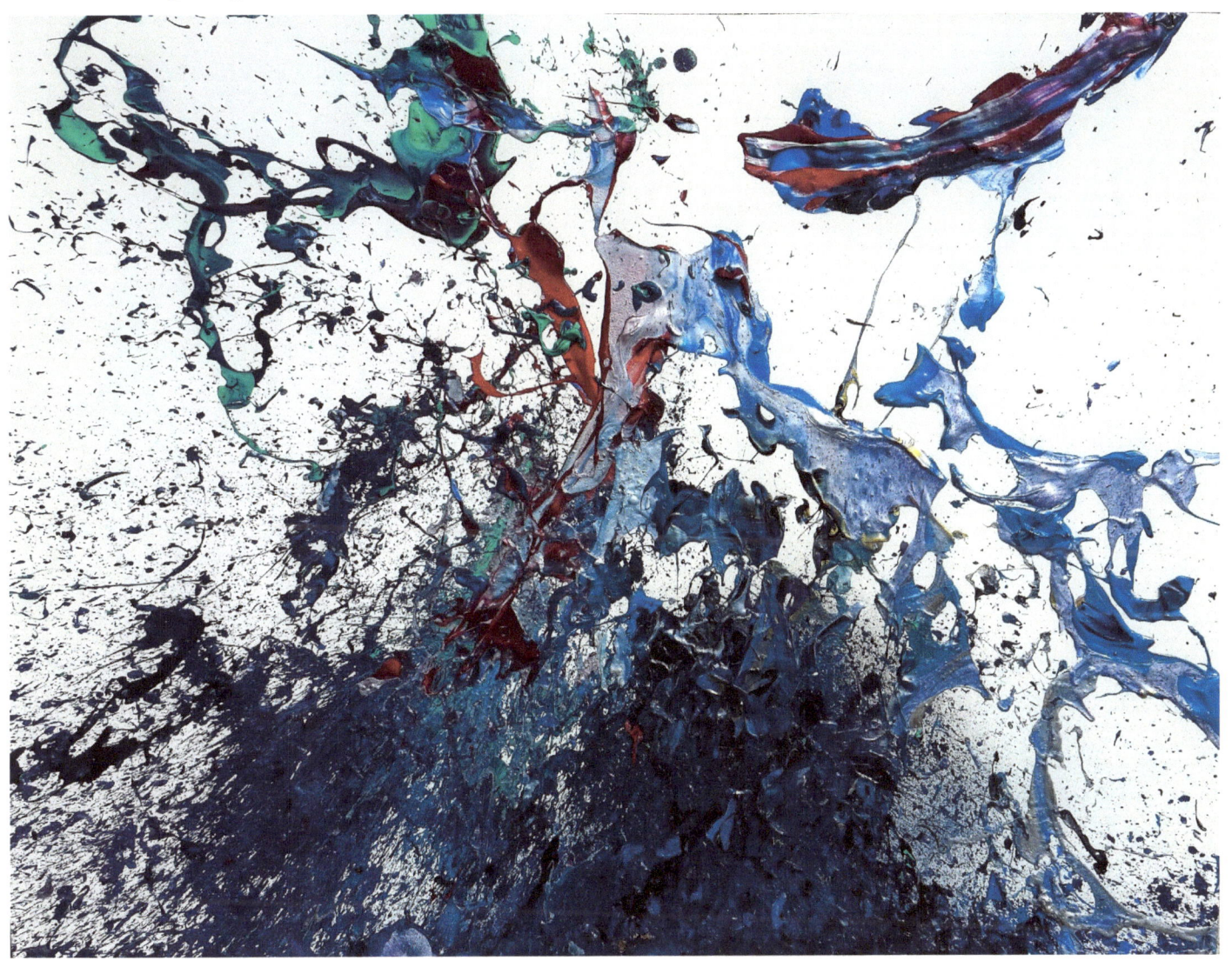

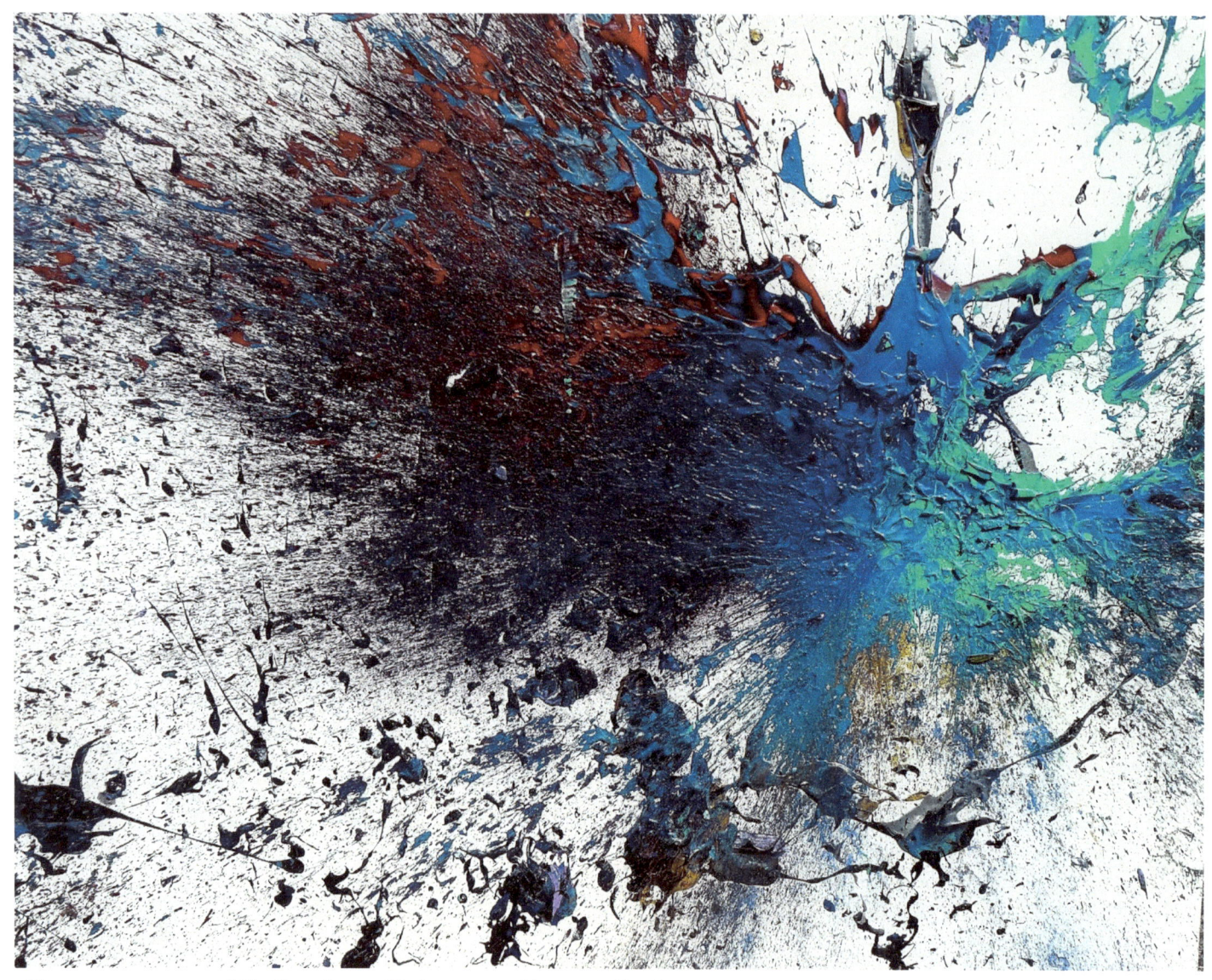

Current page: *Bird takes flight*, acrylic applied to gessoboard with explosives. This piece contains fragments of glass from the container the paint was in pre-explosion.

Opposite page: *Dragon's flight*, the 'ground' was created using the same credit card scraping method employed in *Mending fences*

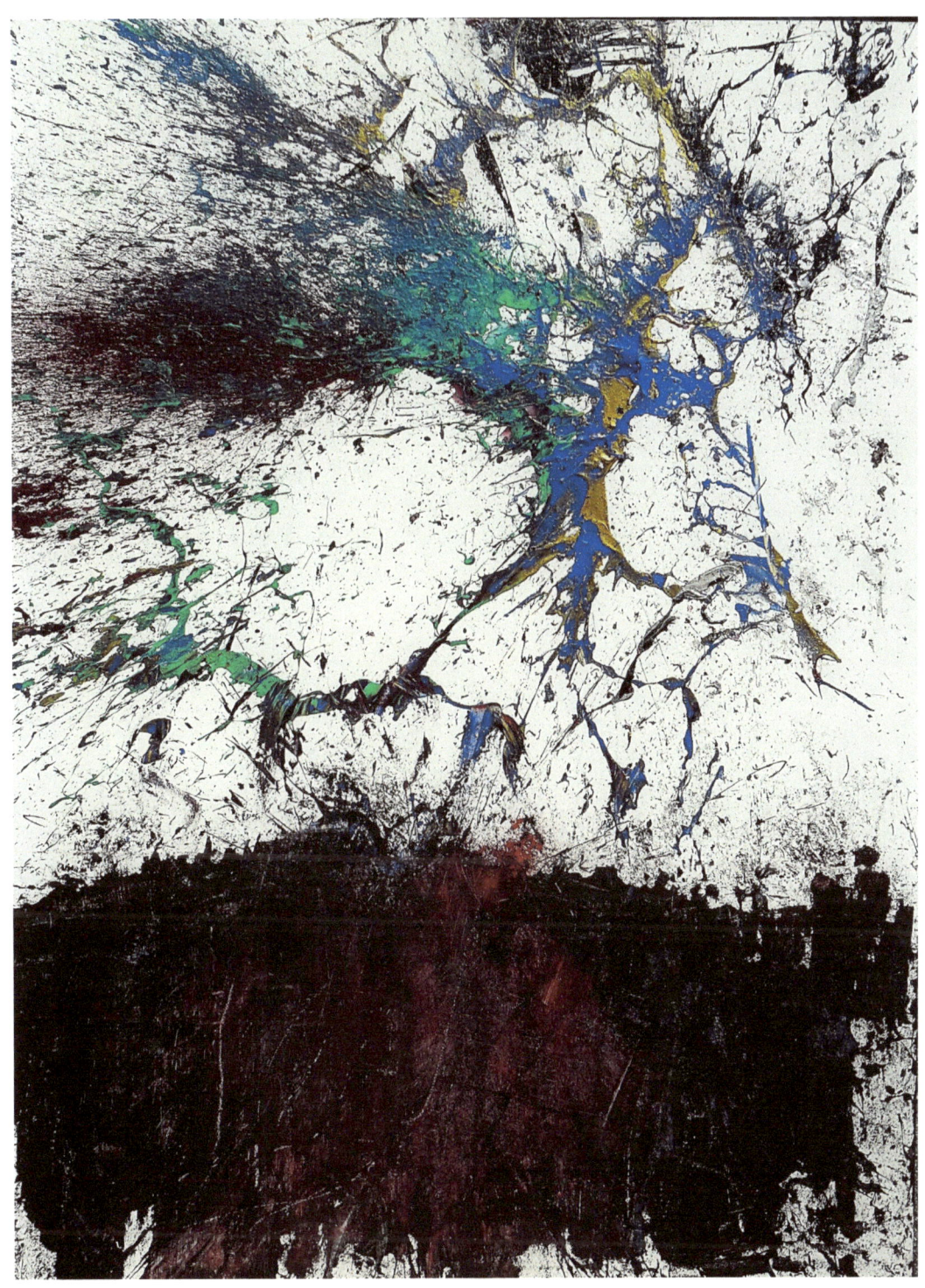

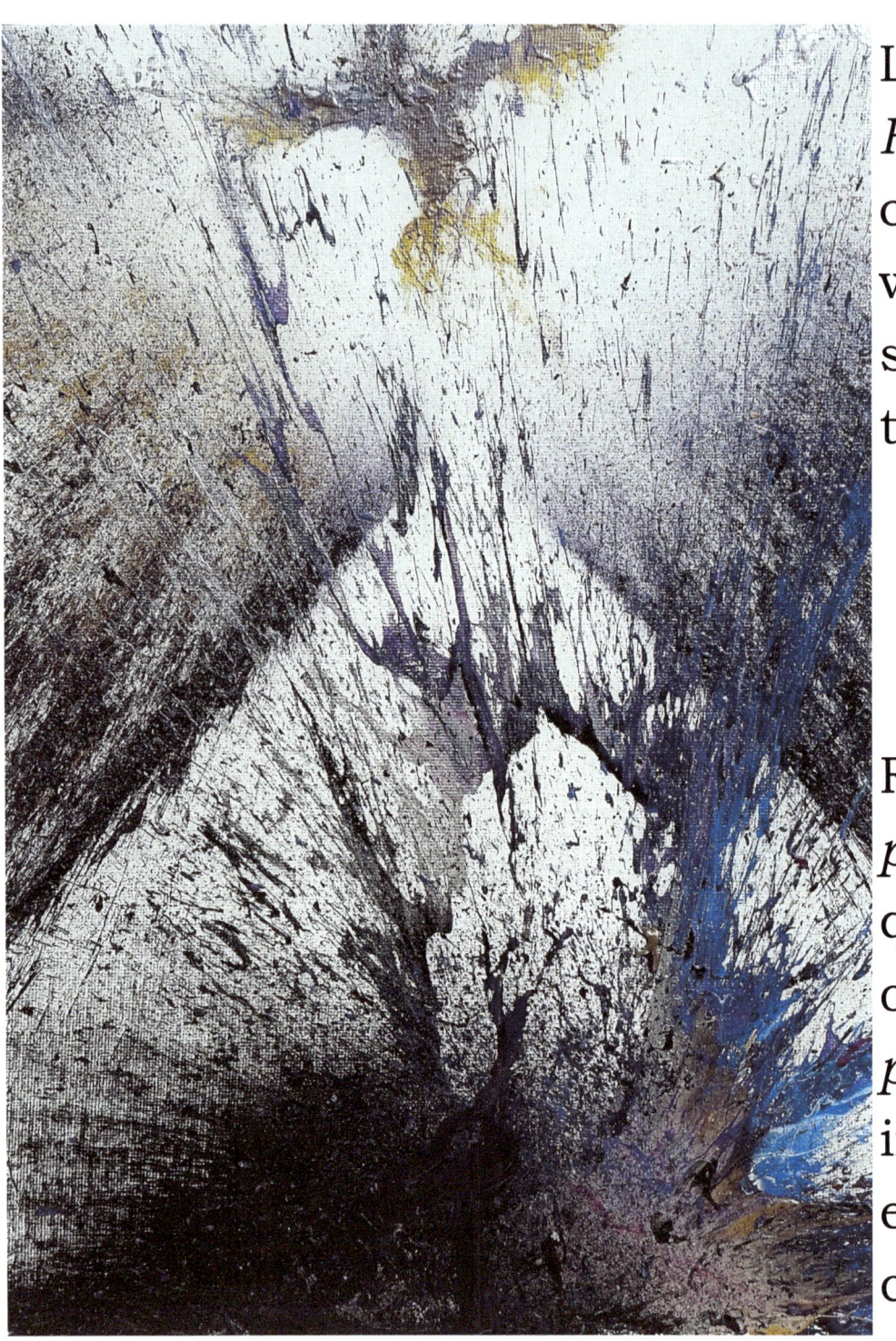

Left: *Osirus Rising*, a rare canvas panel with two explosive applications.

Right: *Blast plate 2*, a sequel to the original *Blast plate*, containing multiple explosive applications

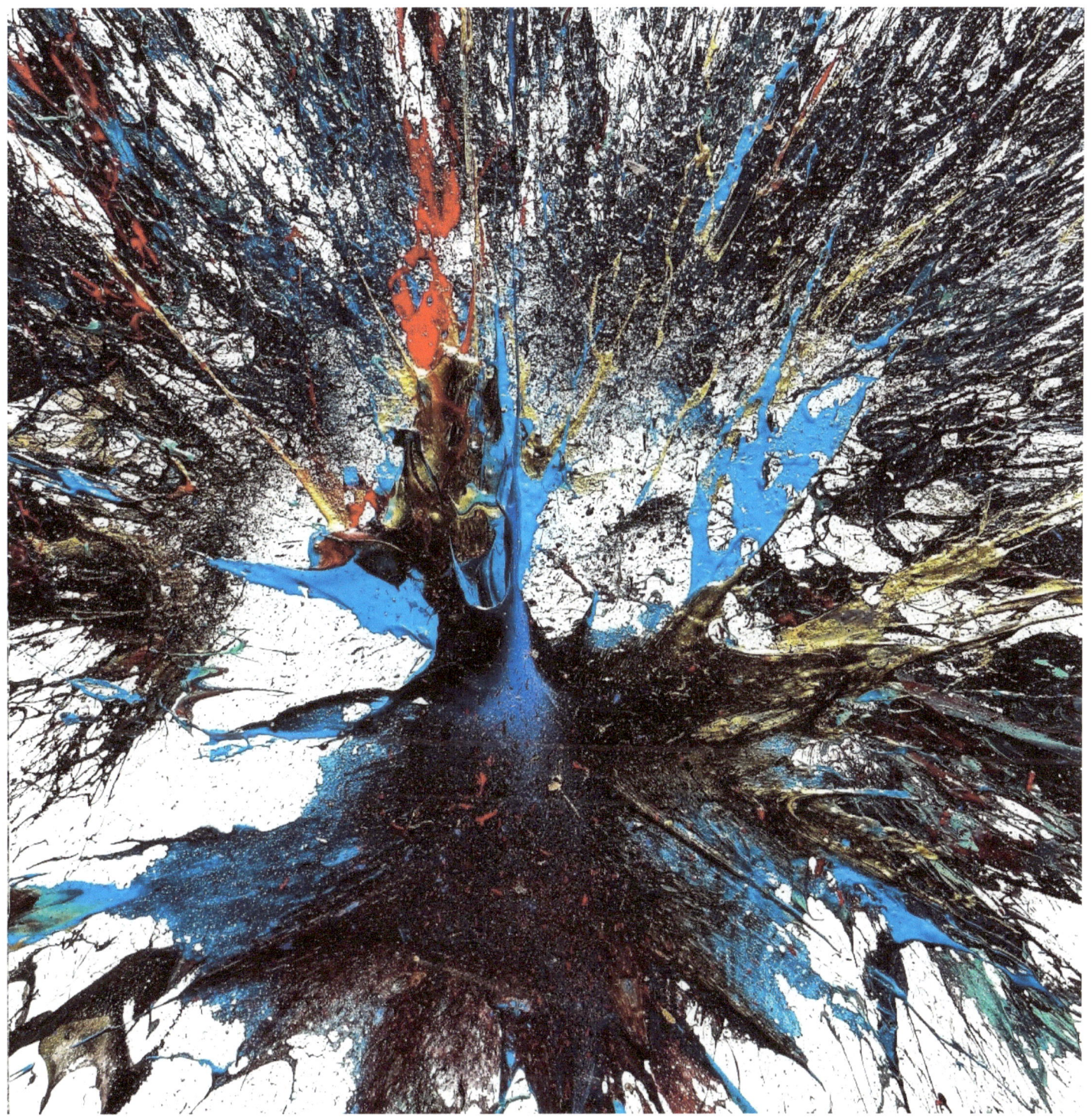

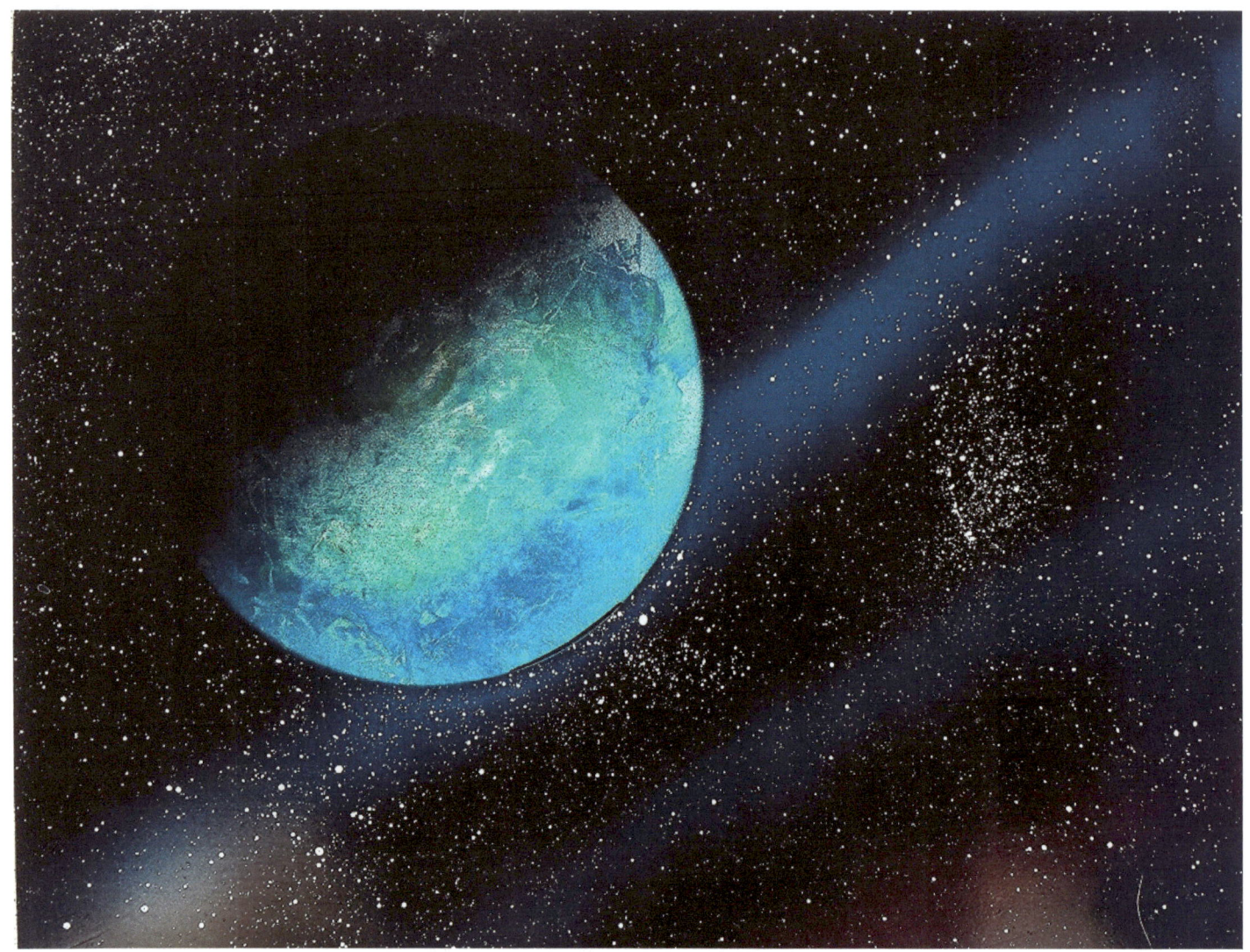

Above: *Earth 2* marks my return to spray paint space paintings. While experimenting with methods for giving the planet texture, I discovered that I could make entire paintings using similar methods. I call these **texturations**.

Opposite page, following two: *Texturesphere, Texturation* and four untitled texturation paintings, respectively.

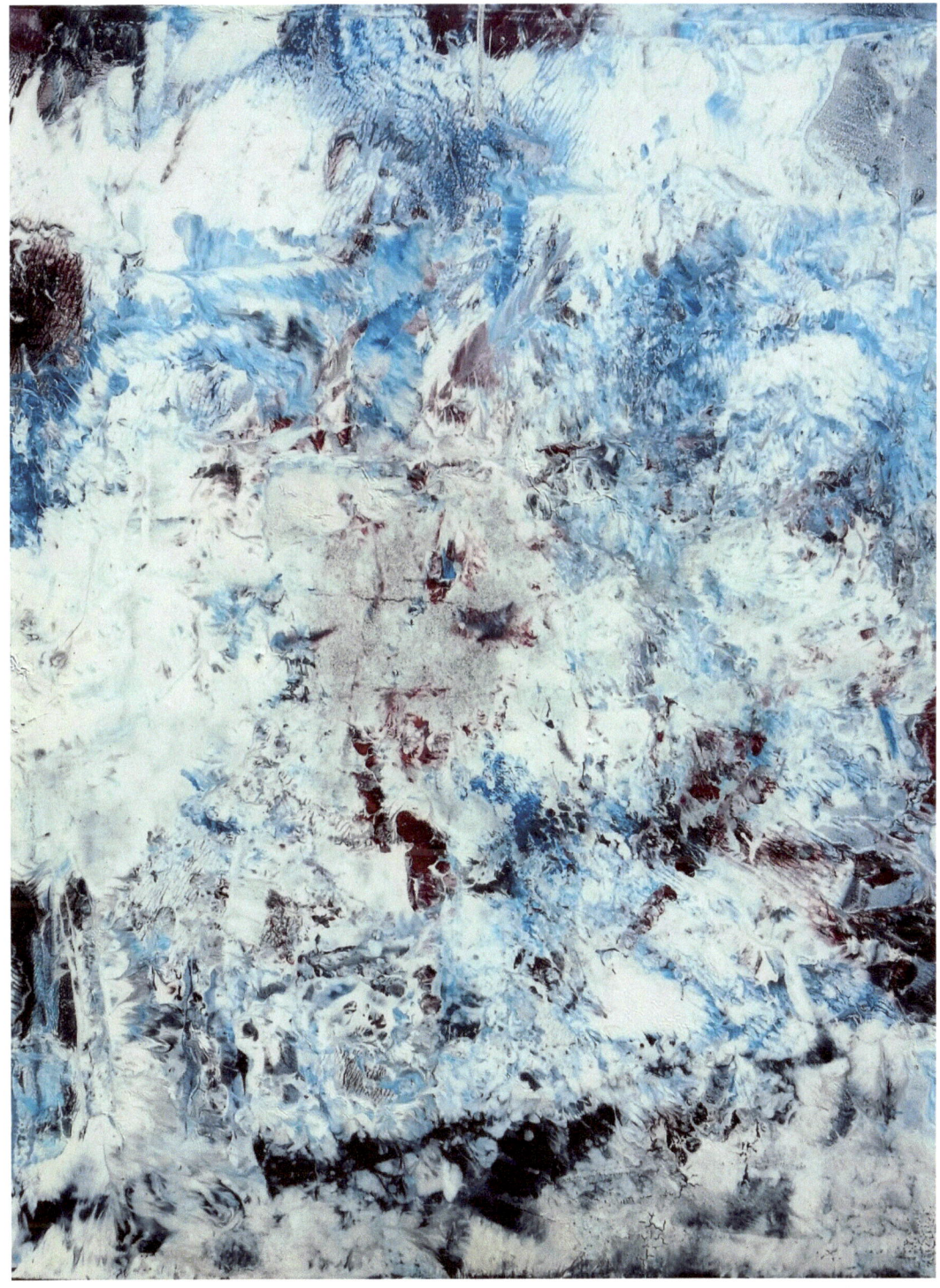

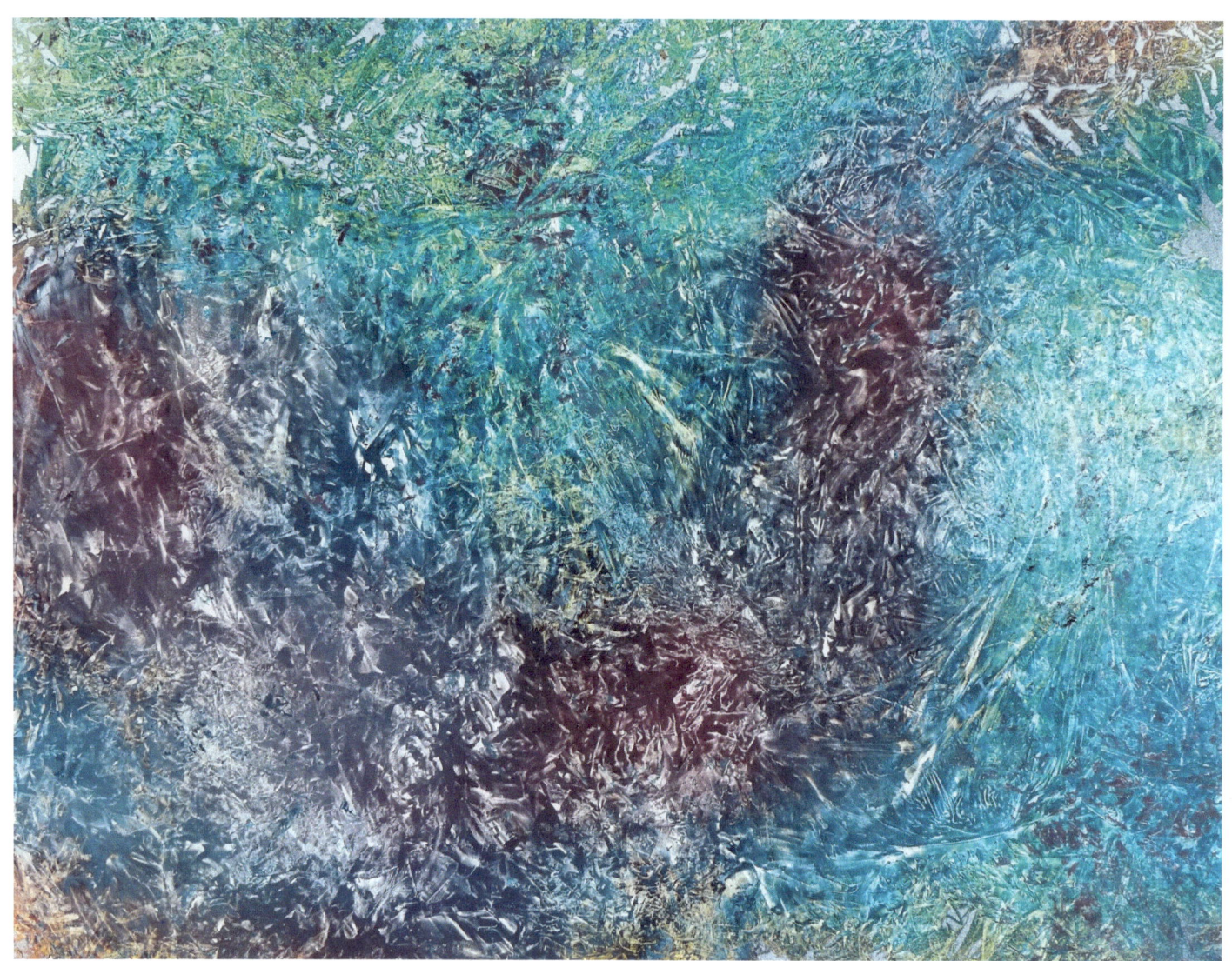

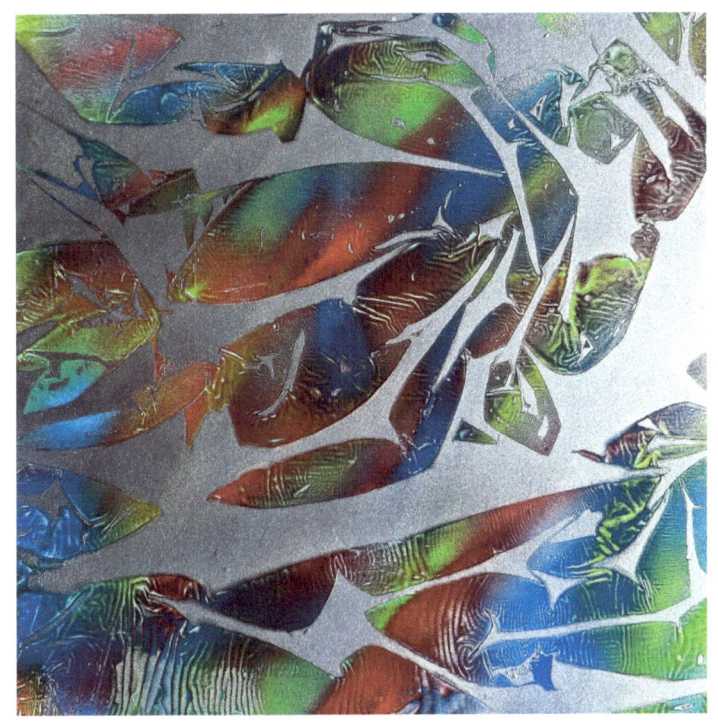
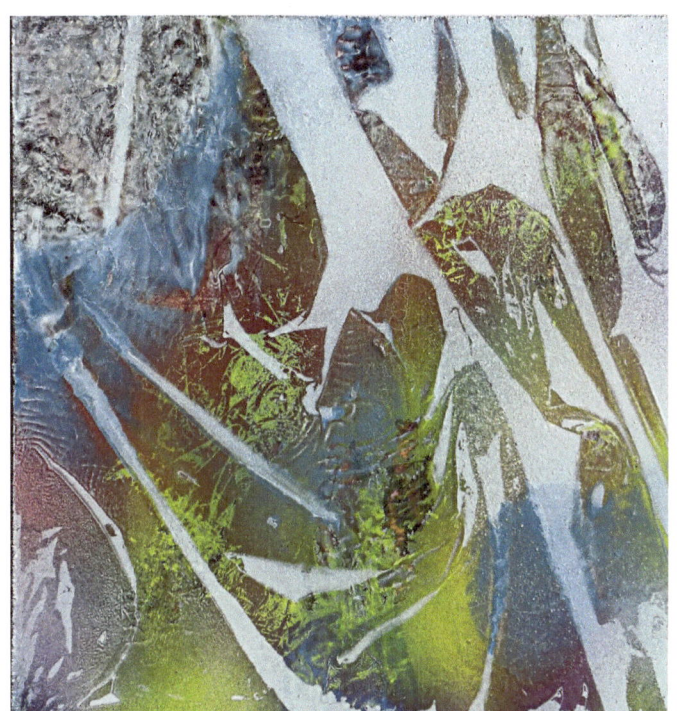
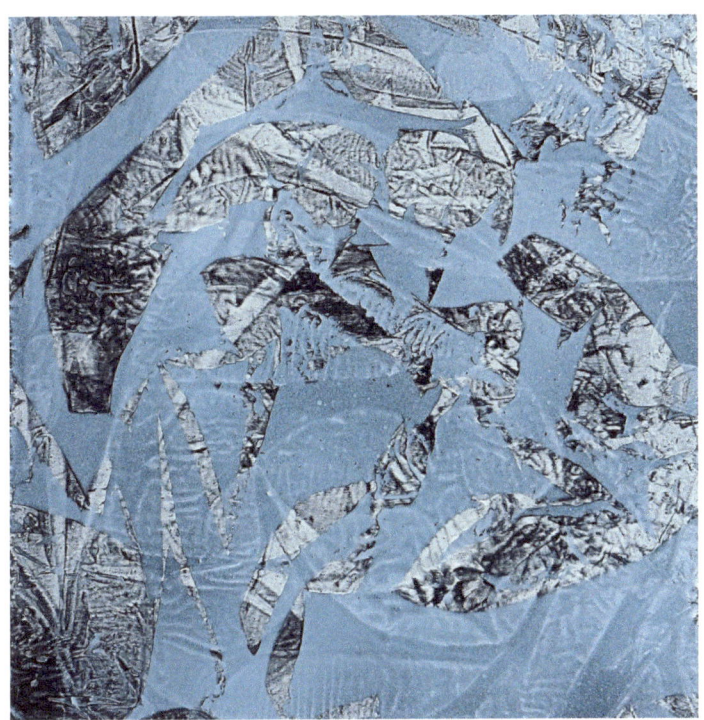
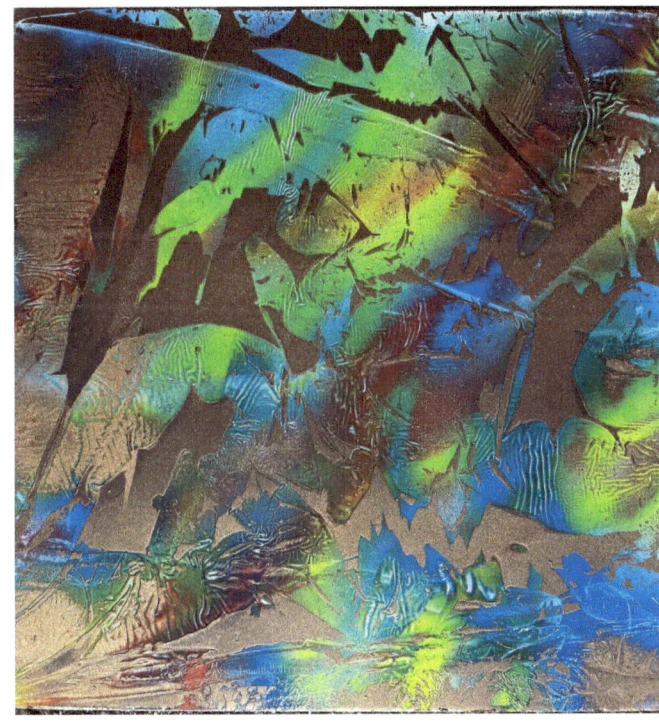

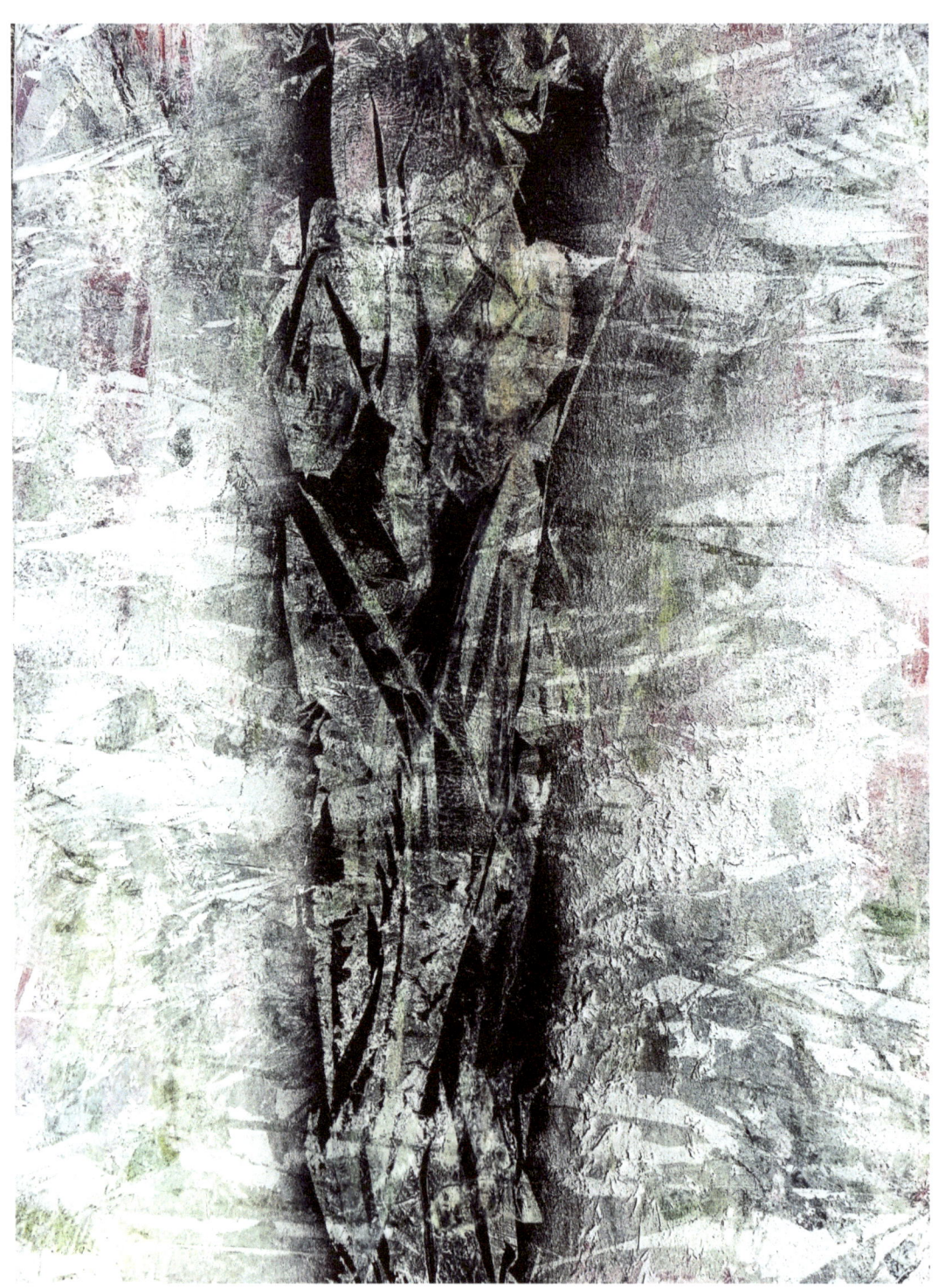

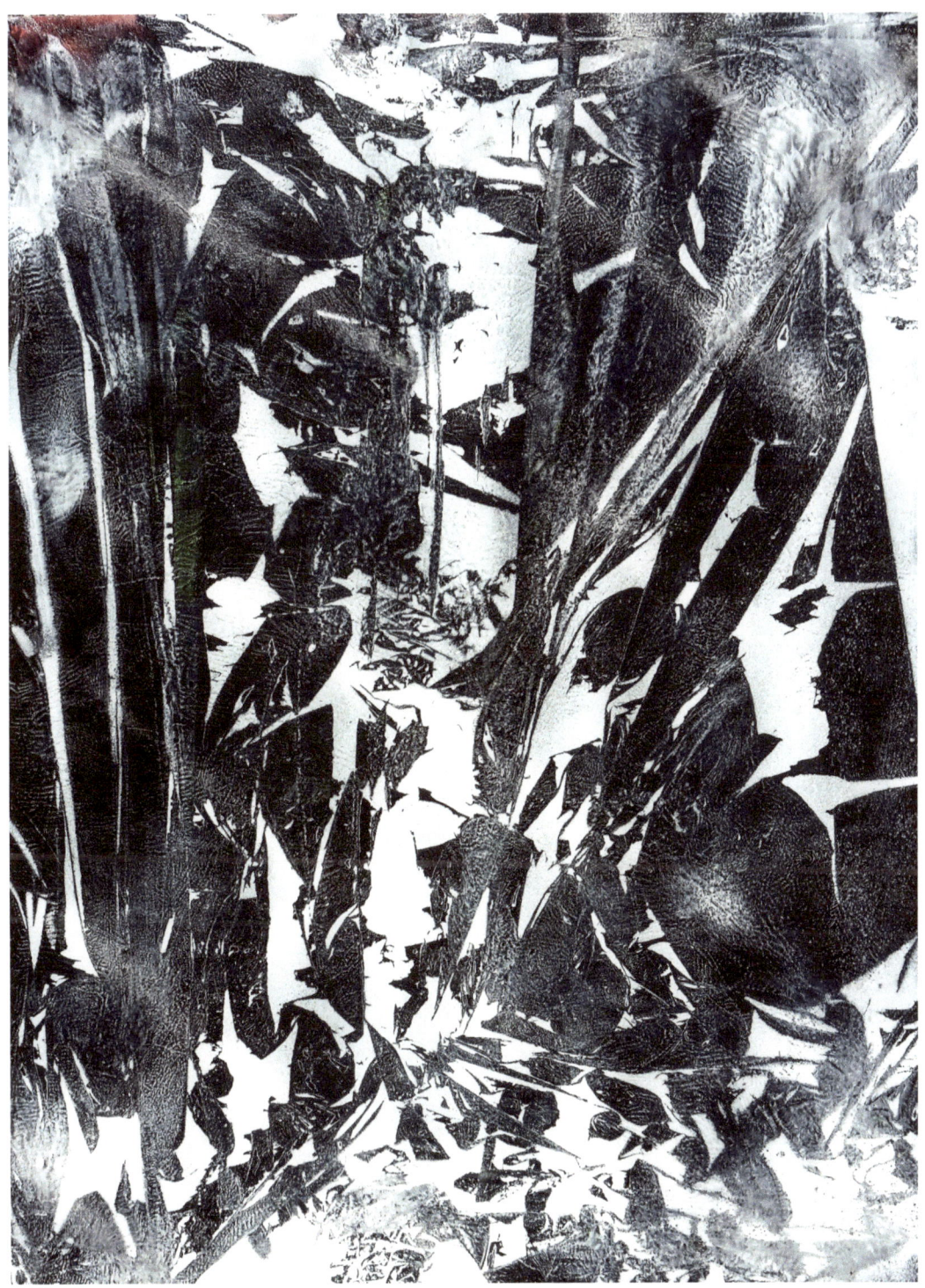

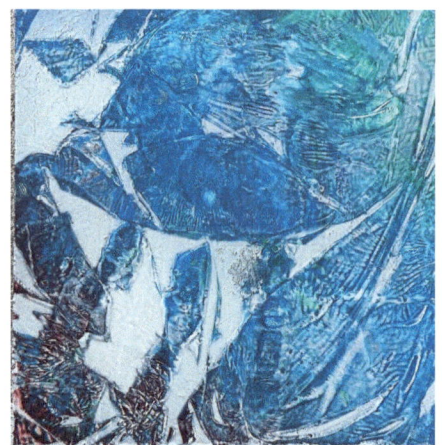

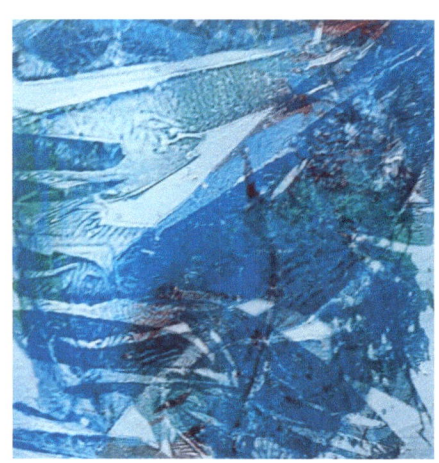

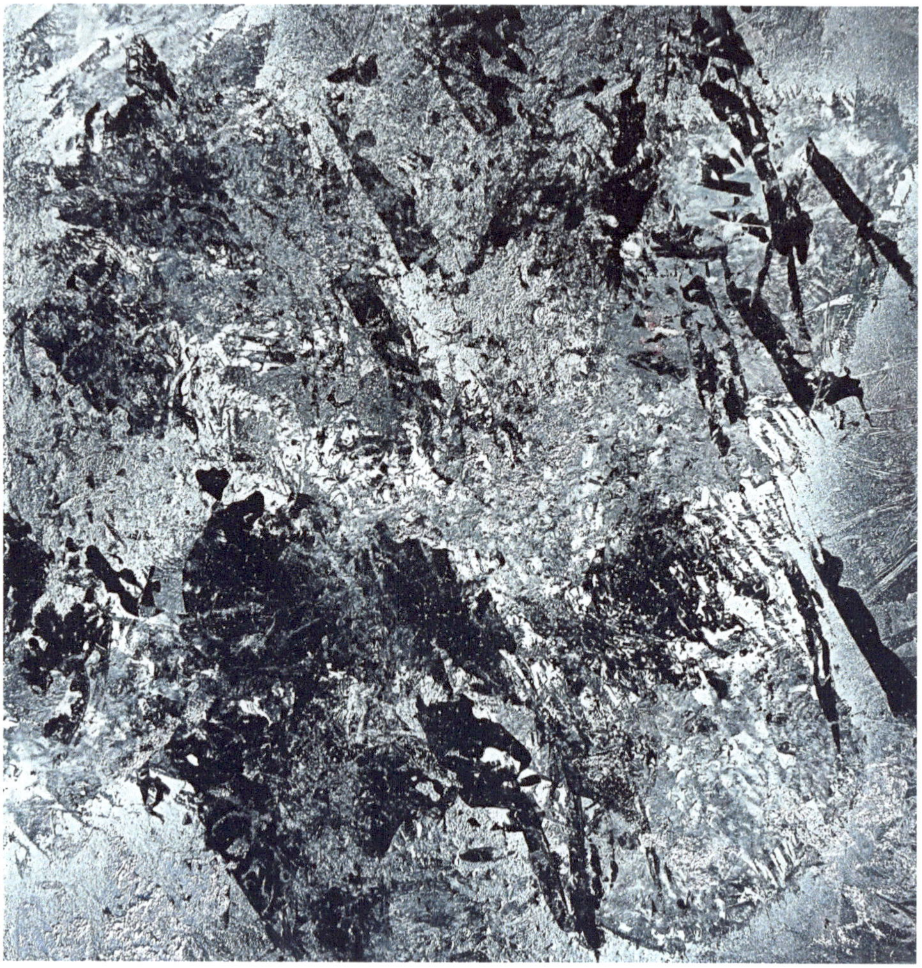

Previous two pages: *Newsprint* (L); *Night path through a snowy wood* (R)

Current page: *Hidden Face* (top left), *Miasma* (right), *Mountain* (bottom left)

Opposite page: *Glacial Spectrum*

All spray paint on gessoboard.

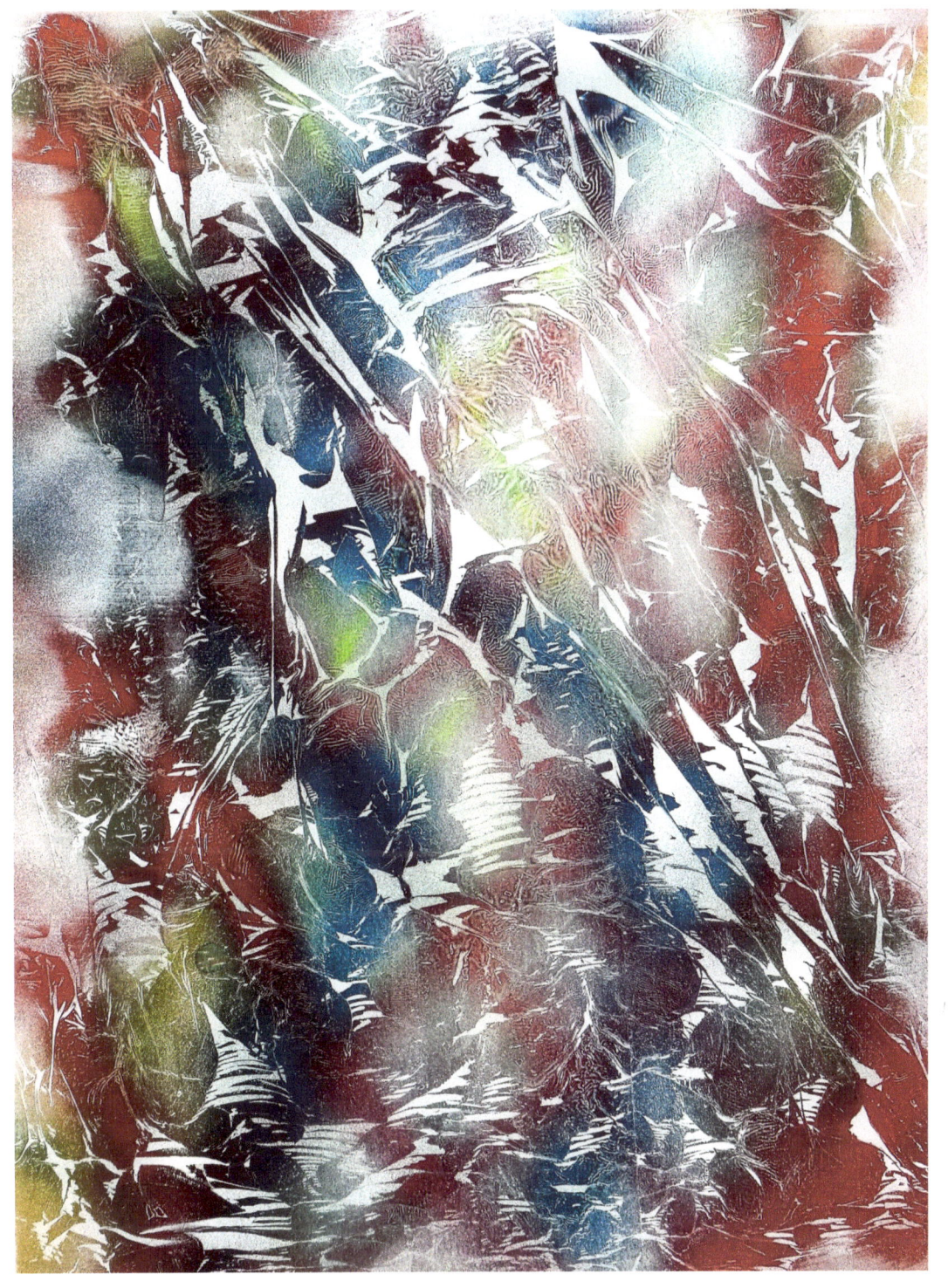

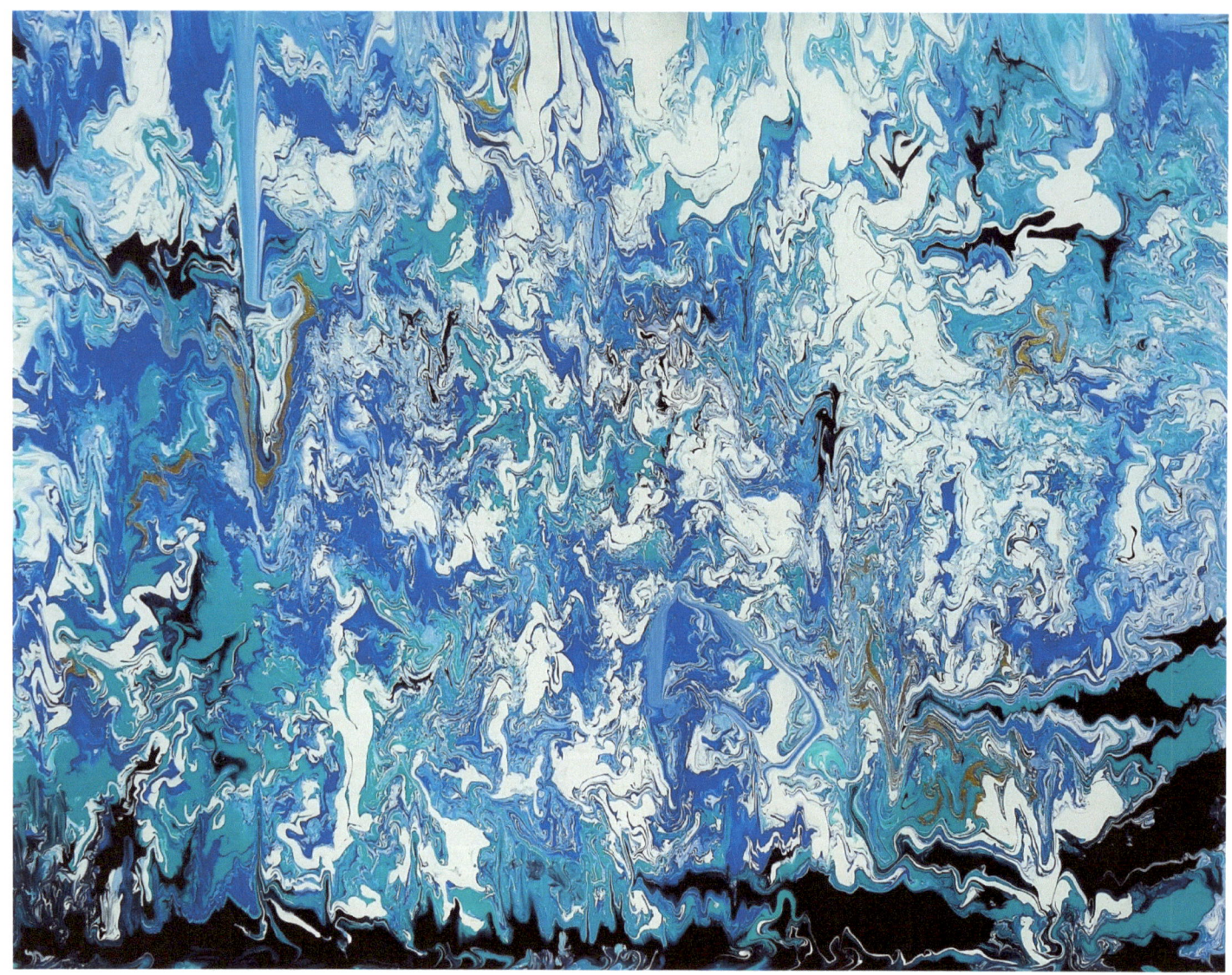

Current page: *Blue marble*, one of my first experiments with liquid acrylic paint (sometimes called fluid art).

Opposite page: *Rivers*, while much smaller than *Blue marble* made every bit as much of a mess on my art table with all of the overflow.

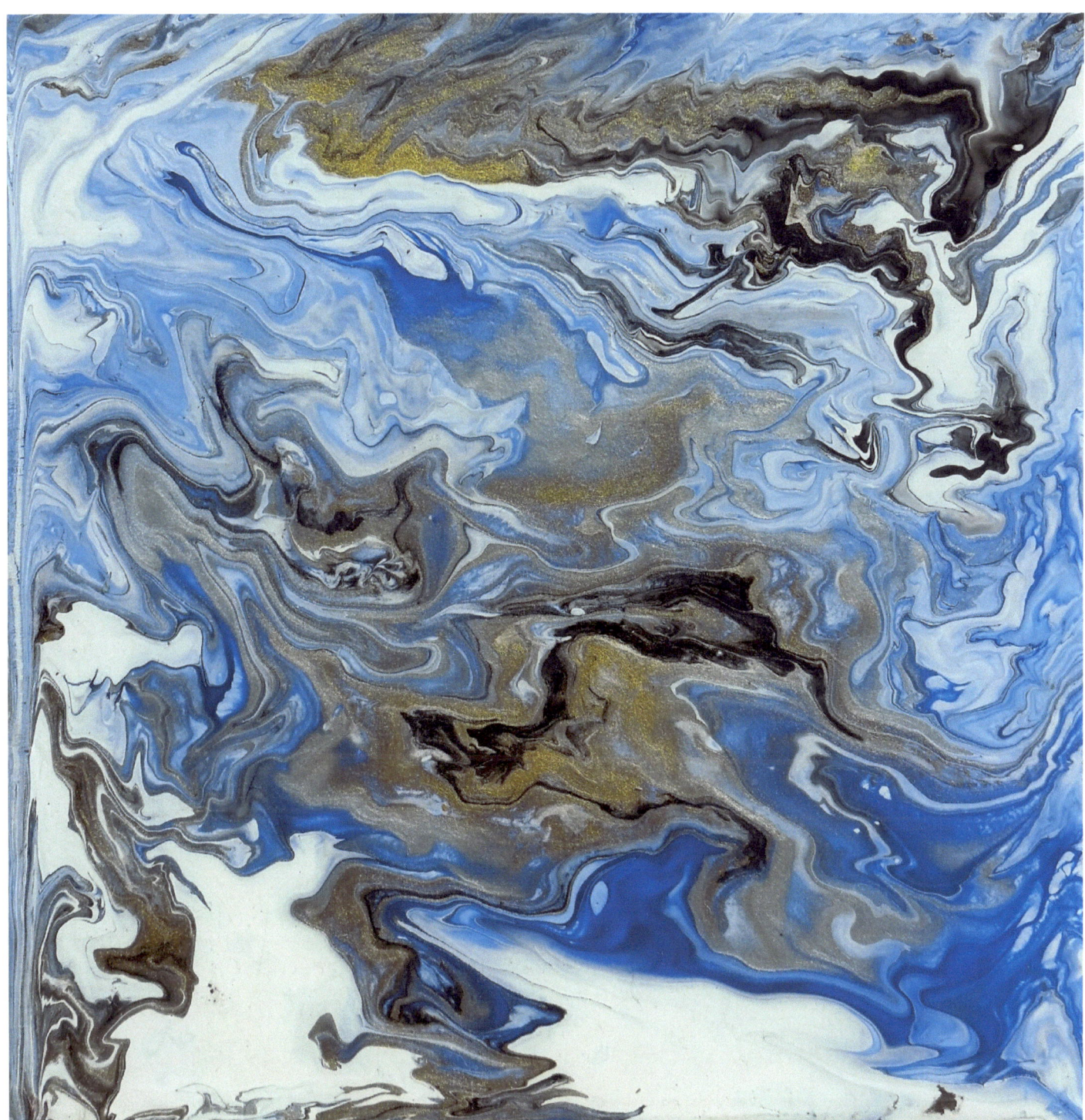

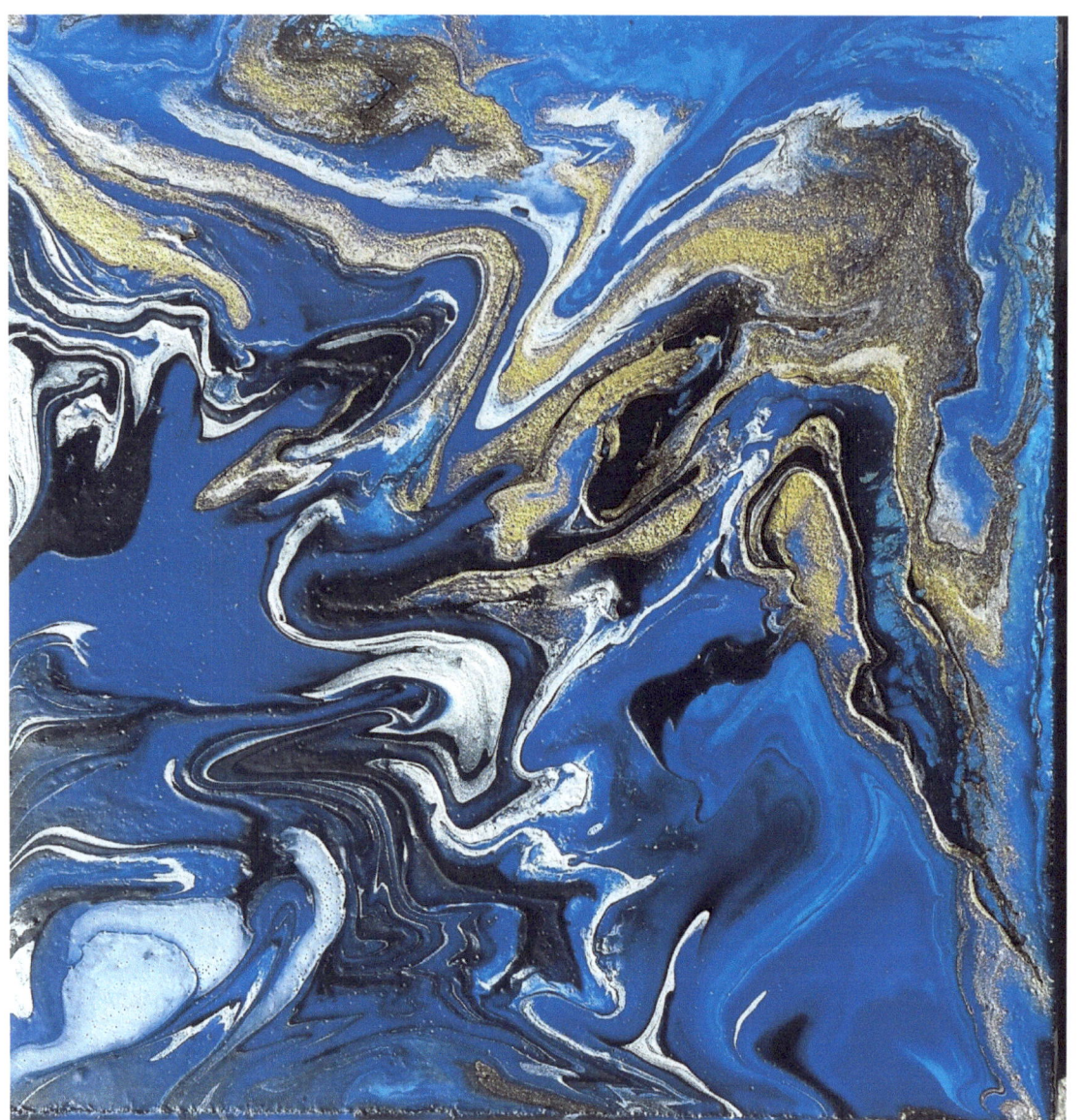

Above: *Swirl's*, liquid acrylic paint on untampered hardboard. The paint textures in this one are a bit more rough because I had mixed the paint too vigorously, creating bubbles in the thinned out paint. I also found something to help reduce the mess and waste of paint...

Below: *Melted Candies* is on the exact same material as *Swirl's*, but instead of pouring the paint directly on the surface, I simply allowed the overflow droplets from *Swirl's* to drip down.

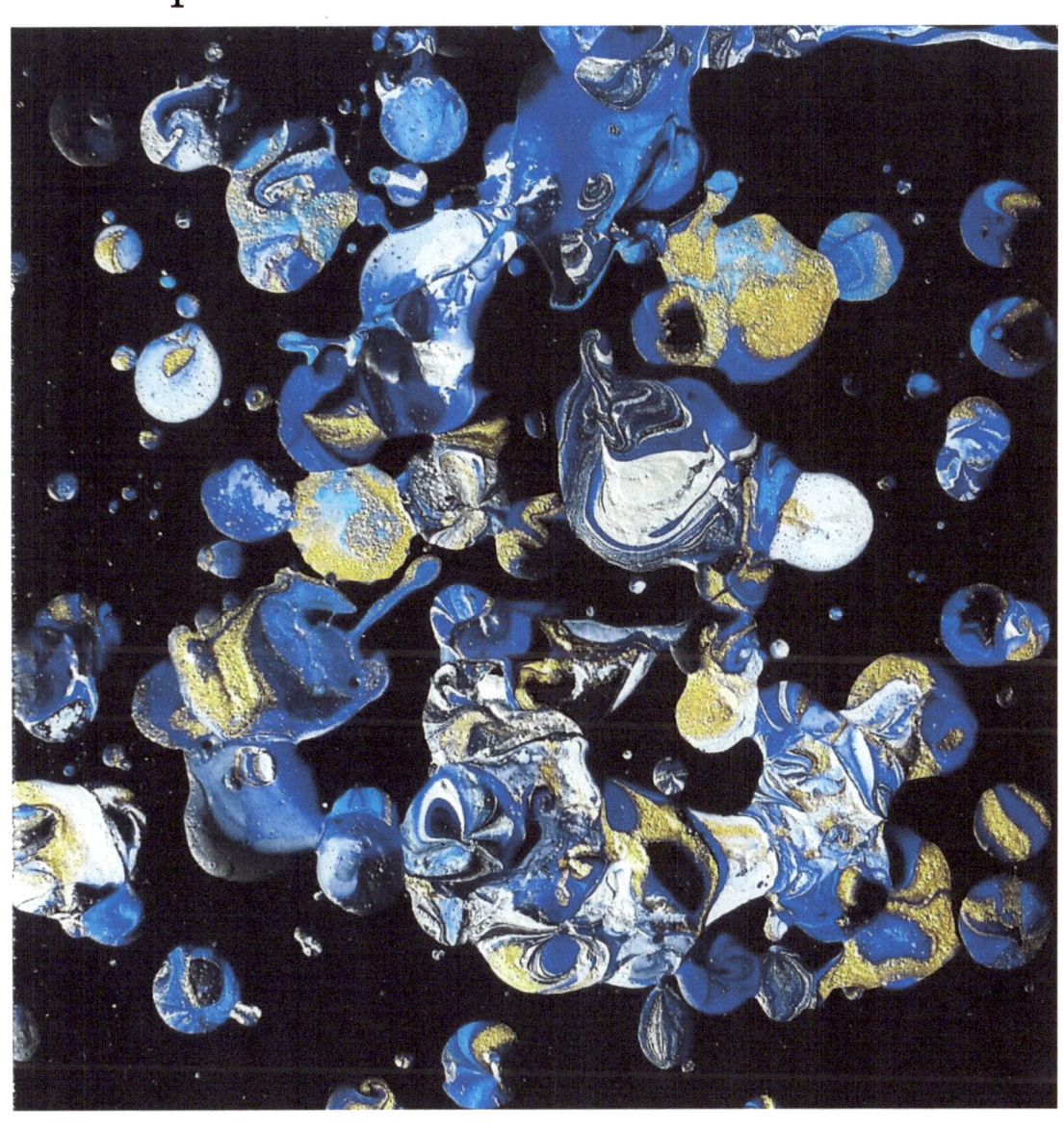

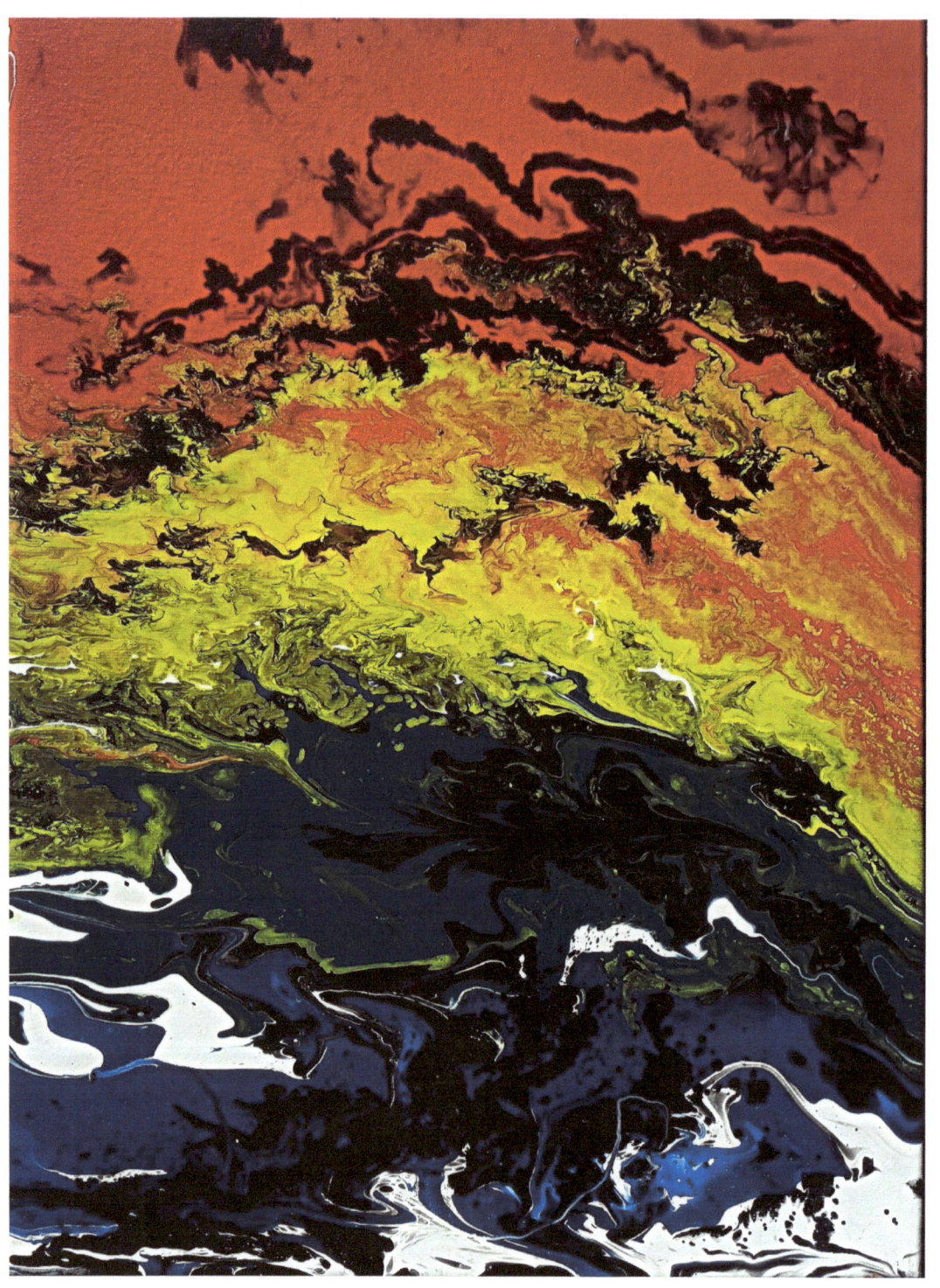

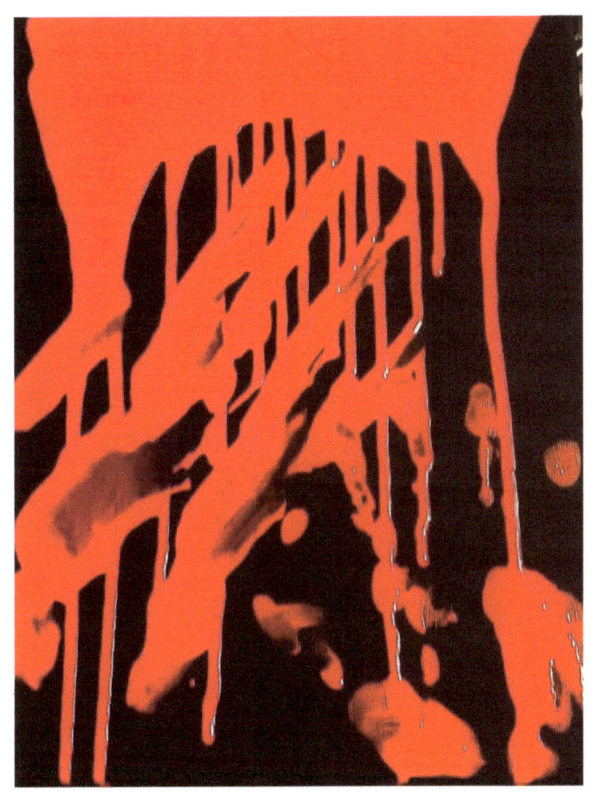

June 12, 2016 was a day that saw a sick man commit a horrible series of crimes, stealing the lives of 49 other people. There was hate and terror and a mentally instability so profound that worlds were shattered.

People I love were suddenly living in fear again, whether for being a member of the LGBTQ community or for happening to share an aspect of religion with the crazed madman.

Our colors run and our fears collide.

Left: *Dangers of silence*

Above: *Complicity*

Both pieces are made with liquid acrylic paint (fluid art) on black stretched canvas.

The killing hasn't stopped, and it won't. Every single one of us in complicit in these crimes so long as we continue to sit and just watch this all unfold like a reality TV show. As long as we change our profile pictures and send up prayers—as long as we continue to hope that **someone else** will magically solve our problems—we all have blood on our hands.

Opposite page: *Some Thing Gold* is a 6x6" untempered hardboard. This piece as well as the pieces on the following pages are a part of the Chaos: black collection, which simply uses deep black backgrounds as the primary surface, allowing for more contrast in the final product.

This particular piece is a fantastic example of how chaotic the process of making these paintings can be. You'll notice that the general pattern is similar to *Cornell's Sun* (and the rest of the Cornell series). The paint looks flatter and almost smudged in comparison, however.

This painting and the piece called *No Thing Gold* (24x48") were created at the same time. *Some Thing Gold* being laid flat, and the taller *No Thing Gold* set vertically perpendicular beside the smaller panel. The glass that was placed on *Some Thing Gold* exploded with such force, that the panel was blown into the air, landing paint side down.

Apparently, my toast doesn't land butter-side-up.

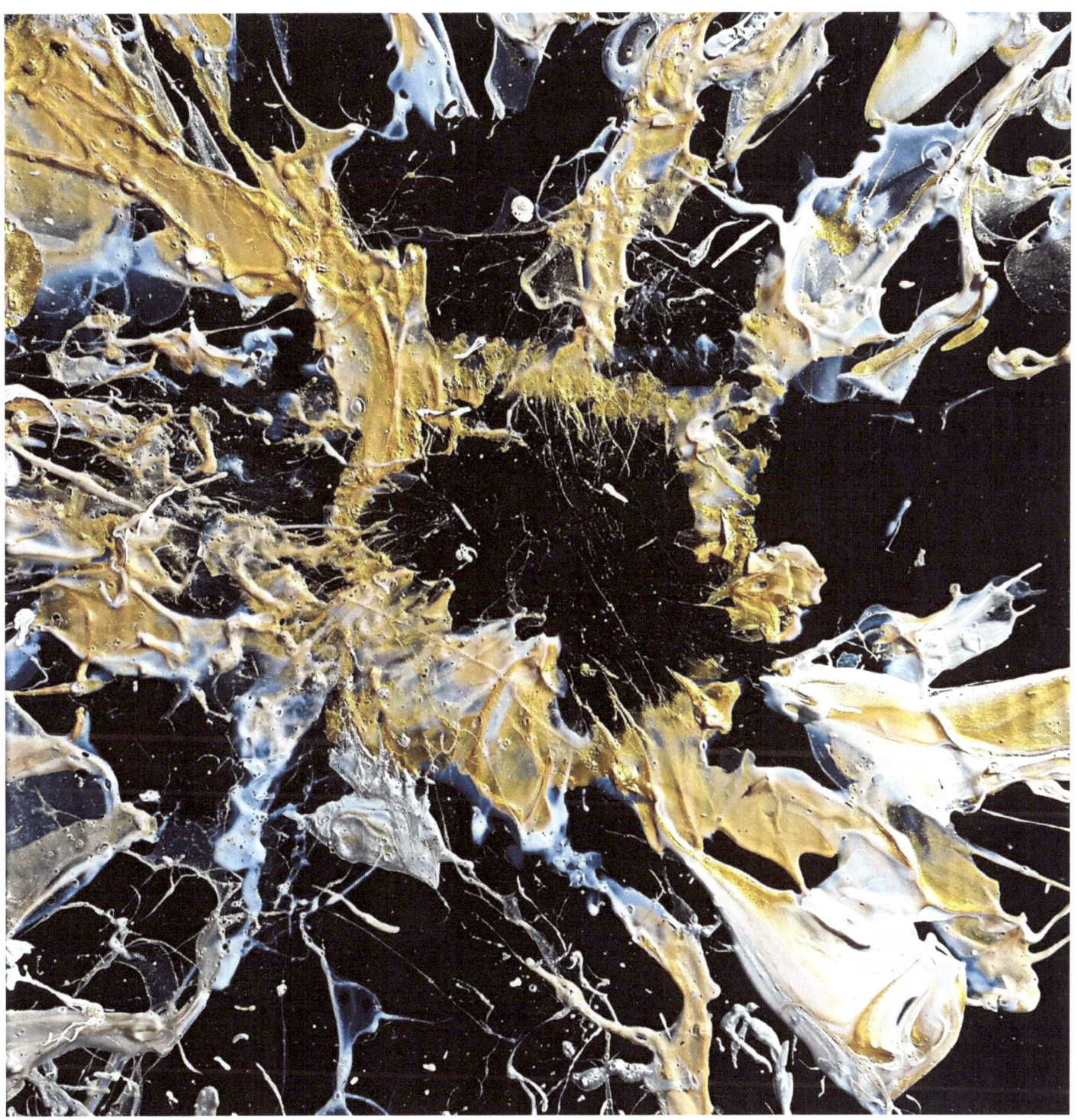

Current page: *No Thing Gold*, 24x48" tempered hardboard with canvas stretcher bars as cradle. Companion piece to *Some Thing Gold*

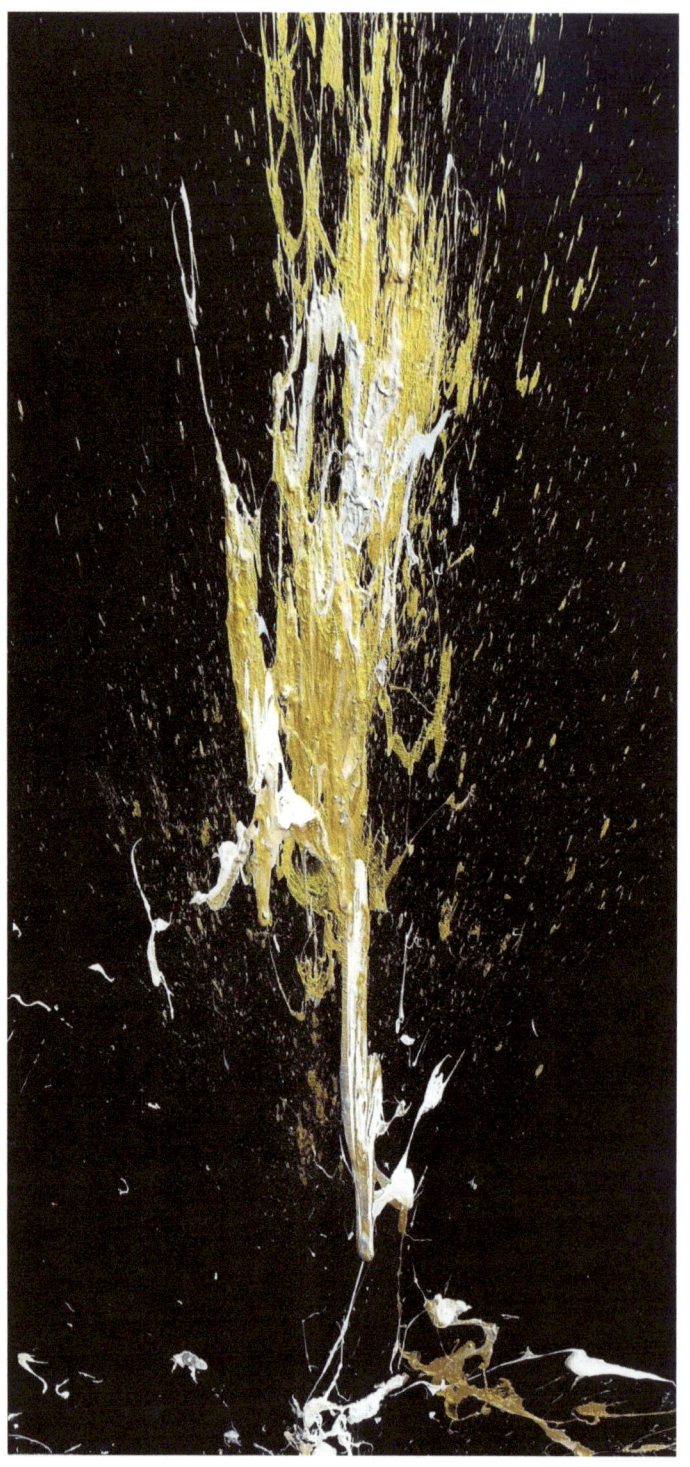

Current page: *April Showers*, 24x48" tempered hardboard with canvas stretcher bars as cradle.

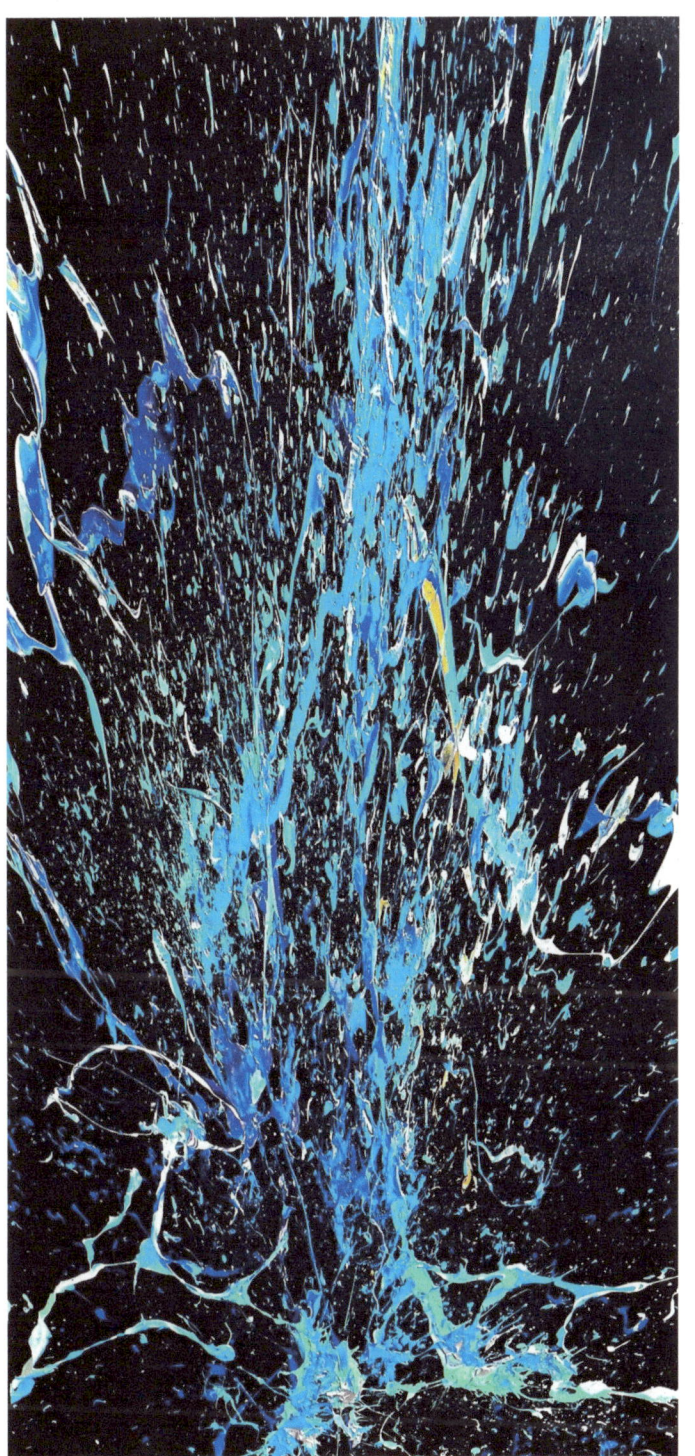

Current page: *Letterbox 2*, 48x24" hardboard with canvas stretcher bars as cradle. Spray paint.

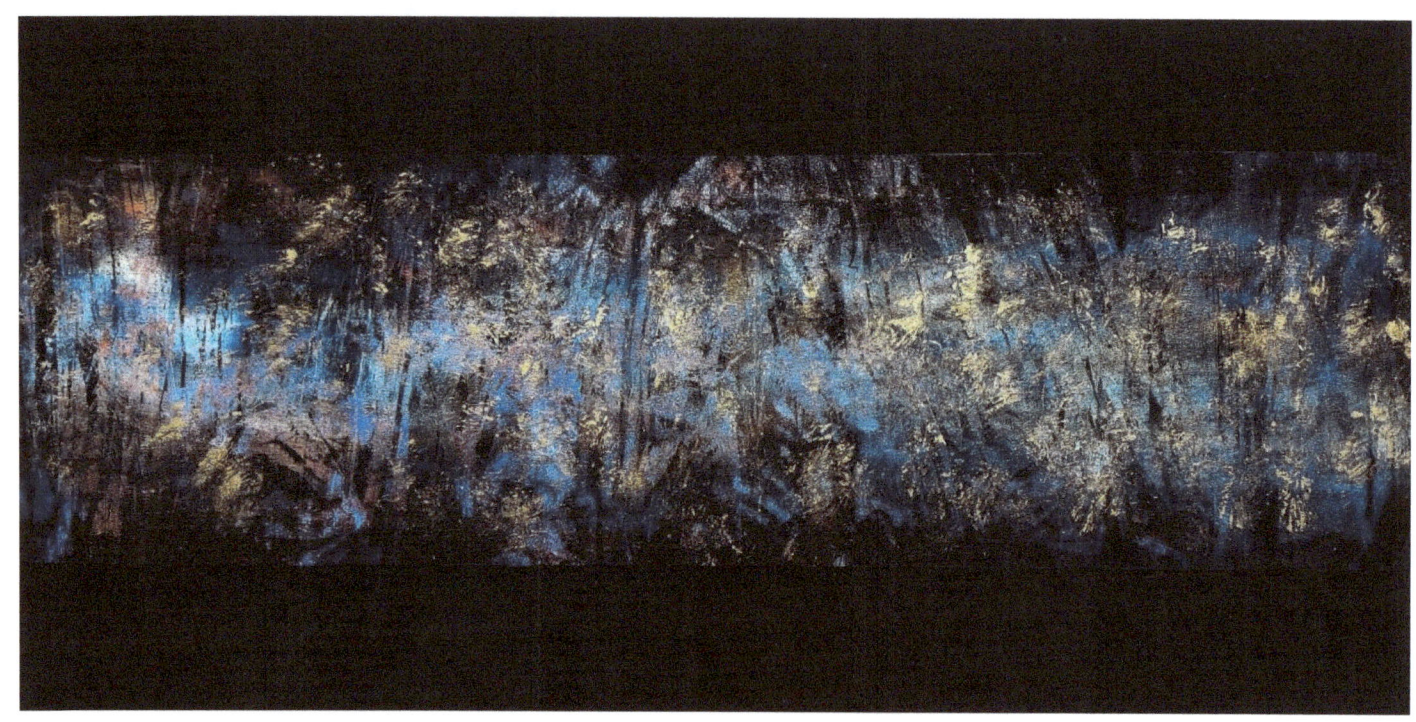

Opposite page: *Blackstar Minoris*, medium density fiberboard with pine cradle.

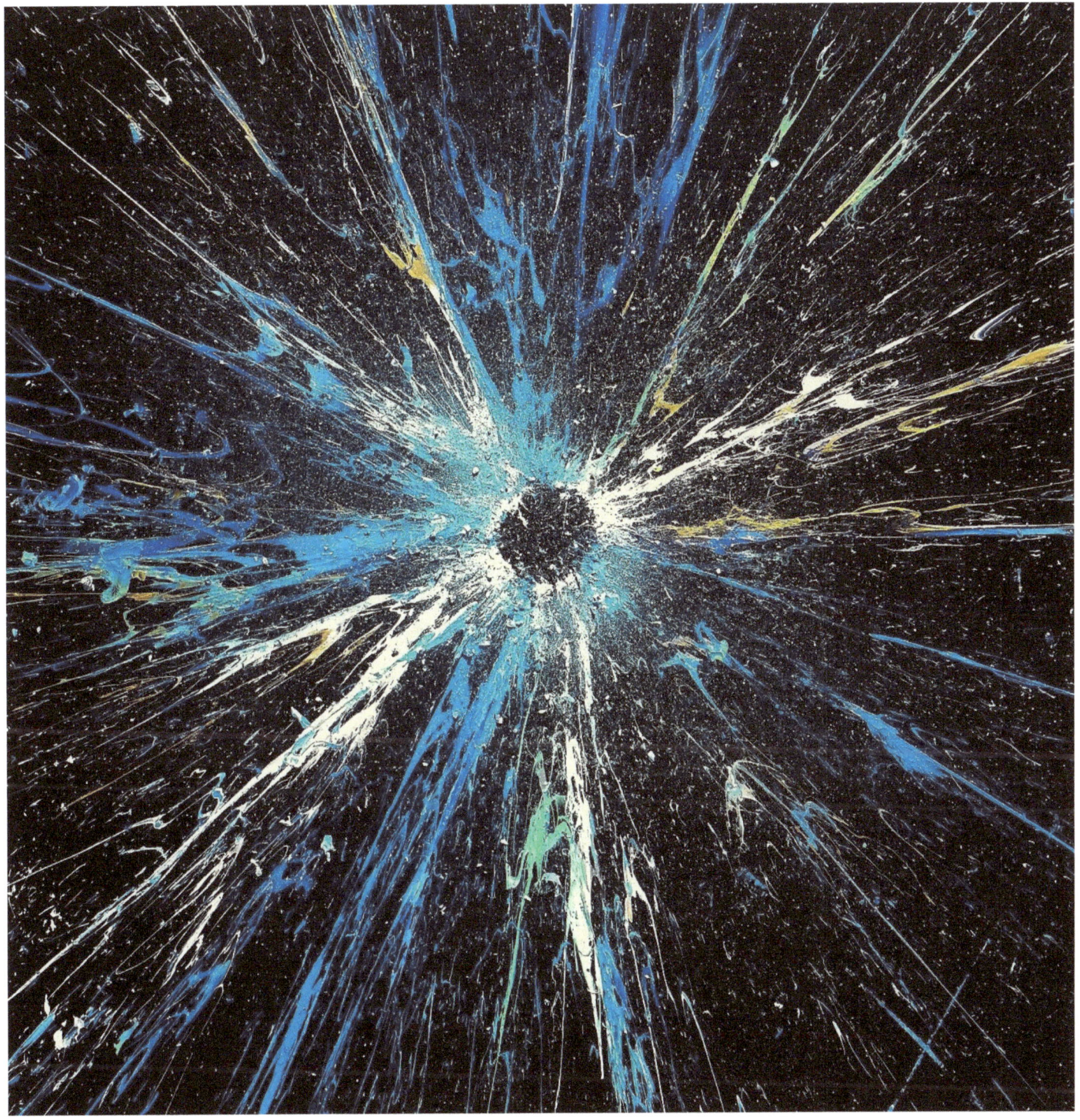

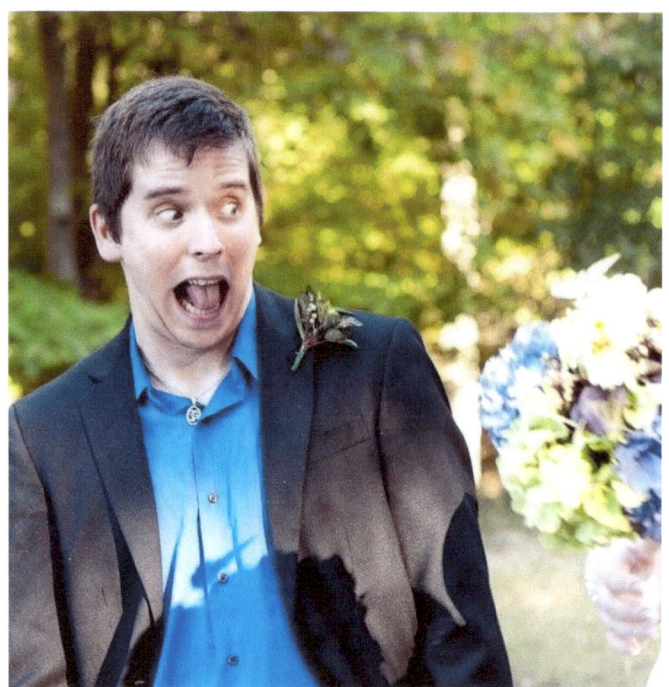

He's probably about 80-90% Muppet.

Artist/Author: Jonathan E. Garner began painting space in 2012 after 30 years of staring at the skies in wonder. Three years later, in the summer of 2015 he started blowing up containers of paint with leftover fireworks after being inspired by the Mythbusters and Mr. Bean.

Based out of Nashville, Jonathan is a lifelong resident of Music City and spends much of his time working and showing art in Murfreesboro, TN. He has shown in multiple Boro Art Crawls and has been featured in the Murfreesboro Pulse and other local/online publications.

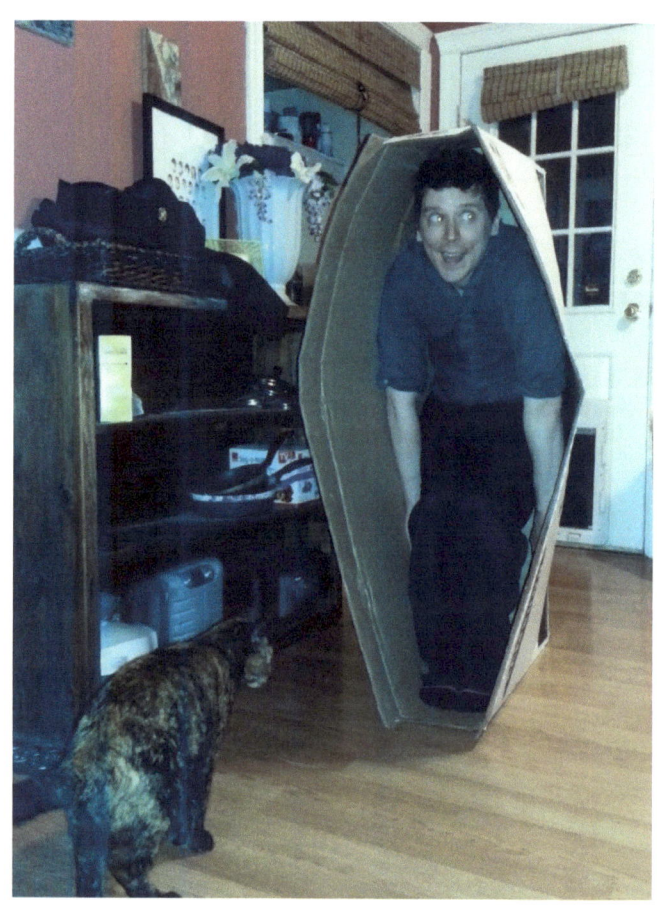

www.ingramcontent.com/pod-product-compliance
Lightning Source LLC
Chambersburg PA
CBHW040417220526
45473CB00004B/1267